The New Return to the Great Mother

ALSO BY ISA GUCCIARDI, PH.D.

Coming to Peace: Resolving Conflict Within Ourselves and With Others (book)
Depth Hypnosis: A Path to Inner Transformation (forthcoming book)
The Four Immeasurables: Meditations on Equanimity,
Loving-Kindness, Compassion and Joy (audio recording)
Preparing for an Empowered Birth (audio recording)
Sacred Drums for the Shamanic Journey (audio recording with Laura Chandler)

The New Return to the Great Mother

Birth, Initiation, and the Sacred Feminine

Isa Gucciardi, Ph.D.

Sacred Stream Publishing

San Francisco

Sacred Stream
PUBLISHING

Sacred Stream, San Francisco, 94127
(415) 333-1434 | info@sacredstream.org | sacredstream.org

Printed in the United States of America

10 9 8 7 6 5 4 3 2 1

Ordering Information:
Special discounts are available on quantity purchases by corporations,
associations, and others. For details, contact the publisher.

Cover Image and Design: Wylie Nash
Interior Design: Cody Humston, Simone Kershner
Editors: Laura Chandler, Melanie Robins

"I Can Feel You" by Laura Chandler, © ℗ Lulu Bucket Music, 2005
Reprinted by permission.

ISBN: 978-0-9898554-2-6

Library of Congress Control Number: 2021933312

This book is dedicated to the Earth.

I can feel you trying to be born
I can feel you like a storm
Little twister making a fuss
Rising up from the dust

I can feel you inside of me
Tossing and turning endlessly
We don't know just what's begun
We won't know until it's done

I can feel you like some fate
All that pushing still you're late
You're just yearning to be free
Still not sure what you'll be

In the blinking of an eye
First we're born and then we die

I can feel you trying to be born
I can feel you like a storm
Little twister making a fuss
Rising up from the dust

Rising up from the dust . . .

- Laura Chandler, "I Can Feel You"

CONTENTS

FOREWORD

The power of women, specifically mothers, has long been honored and revered by our species. Only in recent millennia have the feminine and the Divine Feminine, or Great Mother, been denigrated and undermined in the dominant culture, driving much of her honoring underground.

Isa Gucciardi's book joins the cultural flow toward the restoration of a matrifocal way of being. Respecting the cyclical nature of the world, of life generally, is part of the needed shift. Flourishing societies and a thriving planet require the honoring of mothers and mothering, the grounding of all our lives.

As bodies of energy, we resonate with those around us. Resonating to universal energies is much like wisdom-seeking generally: thinking distracts from being, from being present and from being wise. Successful birthing and mothering are about being, being with others, being in touch with universal spiritual energies. Surrounding a birthing mother with supportive energy—from birthing songs to loving touch—allows mother to entrust herself and baby to a transcendent primal state, attentive to the flow of being, enabling her to bring baby into the world without too much stress.

Baby resonates with mother before birth, taking up her moods biochemically, affecting growth. After birth, baby expects mother and other responsive caregivers to provide the patterns for growing outside the womb. Whereas in the womb, baby's needs were met without effort on baby's part, outside the womb the baby must learn to breathe with the lungs, to feed at the breast, to accustom herself to changing temperatures and body positions. To provide a resonating presence, caregivers at first must be calmly attentive and supportive while baby works things out during the first sensitive hours, days, and months.

Isa brings us the stories and insights of a journeyed practice, millions of years old. A practice of partnership. Mother and child. Mother, child, and others. Our species' evolved nest is all about companionship care through soothing perinatal experience and breastfeeding for the young, and through affectionate touch, social support, play, and nature connection for all ages.

According to a Hawaiian story, each child is a bowl of light. Fears and hurts are stones that collect in the bowl, blocking the soul-light of the child. When a child is not honored, not provided loving presence, stones accumulate. In adulthood, it can take a great deal of work to empty out the stones and restore light to the bowl. Isa's work shows us how to support the bowl of light in both mother and baby.

Isa guides us into new-ancient ways of understanding ourselves as persons, women, mothers, daughters. Take the journey, and be rewarded.

Darcia Narvaez
Professor of Psychology Emerita
University of Notre Dame
Host of EvolvedNest.org

NOTE TO THE READER

The impetus for writing this book was literally born of my experience of giving birth. I did not know it at the time, but it was an initiation, one that would shape me in unexpected ways. It has led me to want to better understand the power of initiation and what it offers us in our modern era, and to share what I have learned with those who may find it beneficial or comforting, particularly those embarking on the birthing process. I am deeply aware that initiation is not limited to women, women's bodies, or women who give birth. Rather, initiation is a human experience, one we each meet on our own terms.

The lens through which I have chosen to look at initiation and the connection to the Great Mother in this book is specific to my desire to help people going through the experience of giving birth. However, the book is also for women who choose not to give birth, trans and non-binary people, and men who want to understand the initiatory experience and connection to the Great Mother through the traditional biology of the female body, or who want to assist someone going through the initiation of childbirth. Even though the book is specific to birth, my hope is that the glimpse it offers into the universal power of the Great Mother will be felt across gender and biology.

On a different note, please be aware that this book is intended as an informational guide; it is not a substitute for professional medical care or treatment.

Regarding Gender Terminology

Oftentimes language fails us. I say this from a place of great respect for words, but also from experience. As a former language interpreter for twenty years and now a teacher, speaker, and writer, words have failed me—or perhaps I have failed them—at times when my intention was to speak with the most grace and care.

All of this to say that I am aware and honor the fact that not all pregnant or birthing people identify as female or would use the term "woman" to describe themselves. While some of us can find a home in the traditional use of gendered terms, many others find them to be restrictive, painful labels that add to the experience of feeling unwelcome.

It is my intention that the words on these pages feel safe and welcoming to everyone. Please know that the terms "woman" and "mother" are used solely for ease of reading and are intended to be inclusive of all who have a womb and are blessed with the ability to carry life within their body.

INTRODUCTION

Open. Open. Open. This is the clarion call of the midwife to the birthing mother as she is encouraged to surrender to the new life moving through her. Childbirth is a sacred initiation that requires our full participation, mind, body, and spirit. We will meet ourselves completely—the parts we like and those we try to hide away in the shadows. But we are far from powerless in this process. In fact, there is a deep and unbroken source of power we can align with for support: the power of the Great Mother.

The Great Mother is the essence of all generative and creative power. Such power is perhaps most evident in nature, where the cycle of life and death is constantly in motion. This is why the Great Mother is so often depicted as an Earth goddess. From Pachamama, the Earth and time goddess of the Andes Mountains in South America, to the ancient Australian aboriginal mother goddesses Kunapipi and Eingana, and even the relatively modern Mother Mary from Christianity, we have been personifying and revering this great source of feminine power for centuries.

I first encountered the power of the Great Mother during childbirth. I have two children, and the birth of the first was very difficult. She and I were in grave danger at times. But it wasn't until labor with my second child began picking up speed that I started having flashbacks from the trauma of the first birth. Just as I was losing emotional and physical steam, I became acutely aware of a brilliant, luminescent, mirage-like presence in the delivery room. This otherworldly light was exuding an enormous amount of power, which I felt directed toward me.

As this power flowed into me, it was like a warm, loving embrace. I quickly stabilized. And as I focused on what I perceived to be a tremendous female presence, she identified herself to me as "the Great Mother." I kept my gaze on this presence for the rest of what turned out to be another challenging birth.

As I skirted the edges of danger once more, I became aware of all the places where the Great Mother had held my daughter and me in the first birth. She had been with us the entire time, even in the scariest moments. I am positive that without the support of this benevolent presence, I would never have had the fortitude to sustain myself, or my children, during childbirth.

The encounter made me curious about this presence. I wondered what it was and whether it worked with others in a similar way. What I have found is that the presence and power of the Great Mother is not unique to me. In fact, I have personally witnessed her at work during the many births I attended in my former role as a medical language interpreter. Without fail, the Great Mother was there to guide and assist each woman as the unique story of her child's birth unfolded. The Great Mother's presence was always unwavering. In some of the most intense situations I could feel her force sustaining the lives of mothers and children just as she had sustained mine.

In order to help women gain direct access to the power of the Great Mother, I have developed a simple meditation I call the Great Mother Meditation. This is a helpful tool for birthing mothers and their partners and for birth attendants and professionals. The simplicity of this meditation allows each of us to encounter the Great Mother on our own terms. We do not have to hold any set of religious beliefs or obey any culturally defined rules to encounter this power. In fact, we are free to perceive the Great Mother in any form that has meaning to us. I use the term "Great Mother," because that was how she presented herself to me.

Since publishing *Return to the Great Mother* in 2013, numerous mothers, partners, and birthing attendants have come forward to share their stories with me and to express gratitude for helping them connect with the power of the Great Mother. Some are continuing to strengthen their relationship with this ancient and ongoing source of power, calling upon it whenever they are faced with situations that require them to step outside of their comfort zone and into a new way of knowing themselves or life.

Within this book, you will read these and other stories about how the Great Mother was there, always supporting—sometimes sustaining—the women and children as they moved through the sacred initiation of childbirth. In this updated edition, I have included information about the importance and power of initiations. While childbirth is the focus of this book, it is just one of seven key steps we take on the path toward personal growth. To assist in your understanding of the stages of your own initiations, I have also included some simple exercises for you to engage with in Chapter 4.

It is through the discussion of the seven initiations of birth, puberty, menses, first sexual encounter, childbirth, menopause, and death that I hope to shed light on the life-altering effects that initiatory experiences can have on us. Like rungs on a ladder, each initiation can serve as a sturdy step upon which we feel supported as we climb upward toward greater awareness and understanding of ourselves and our place in the world.

Unfortunately, in our busy, materially focused culture, the powerful teachings that initiations afford us tend to be lost completely or, worse, disempowering and even traumatic. In these cases, cultivating a connection with the Great Mother is even more therapeutic, so that we may begin to heal those hurt places within us, ideally before entering into the initiation of childbirth.

For too long, our culture has overly valued qualities largely attributed to masculinity, such as assertiveness, competition, and logic, while those related to femininity, like openness, harmony, and sensitivity, have been minimized or ignored entirely. The result is an imbalance in the systems and structures within the culture as well as the disunion of the masculine and feminine aspects within us. These disconnects can negatively affect our relationships to our bodies, our initiatory experiences, and our personal or spiritual growth.

In many ways the disconnection we experience on a personal, interpersonal, collective, and even on a spiritual level manifests globally as a disconnection from the ultimate giver of life, the Earth. Sadly, as a society we are no longer connected to the Earth or ourselves as we once were. Our fast-paced, always moving world discourages these bonds from forming and, as a result, we may carry in our heart a sense of disconnection or separation that we do not understand. This can look like anxiety, depression, or self-loathing. But it doesn't have to be this way.

As we will discuss later on, the body is a template for spiritual growth. And of all the sacred initiations that we undergo, childbirth is one of the most potent in its requirements of us physically, emotionally, mentally, and spiritually, but also in its ability to change us.

My goal is to help prepare every woman for the initiation of childbirth by teaching her to connect with the Great Mother. She came to me and countless others in our greatest time of need and I know she will be there for you or the woman you are seeking to assist as she brings life into this world. The Great Mother is always there. All you need to do is call on her.

May the Great Mother guide and protect you on your journey.

CHAPTER 1: REMEMBERING OUR POWER

"We need to understand that there is no formula for how women should lead their lives. That is why we must respect the choices that each woman makes for herself and her family. Every woman deserves the chance to realize her God-given potential."

— Hillary Clinton

Women are powerful, highly capable beings. Our bodies are the driving force behind much of our abilities and power. For instance, our monthly menstrual cycle regularly draws us inward, bringing us closer to our spiritual selves. The hormonal shifts we experience throughout the month bring us ever-greater awareness of our thoughts and emotions. And our physical form, the flesh and bone we are made of, is able to create and sustain life.

Unfortunately, many women have forgotten what powerful forces reside within us, and we therefore begin to doubt our abilities spiritually, mentally, emotionally, and physically. The root of this distrust doesn't come from within; rather, it is the result of living in a society that does not acknowledge or respect these and other feminine qualities and characteristics. And because the majority of our more recent ancestors also lived in patriarchal societies, distrust of the feminine has been brought forward and repeated over and over again, stamping it onto our collective and individual psyches.

The result is that many of us have trouble trusting our power. We may even feel bad about some of our more feminine qualities, like emotionality and sensitivity, or reject our bodies and their many urges, needs, and functions. All of this external messaging has distorted the way we see and experience ourselves, not unlike a reflection in a funhouse mirror. But this distortion stretches well beyond women because there is feminine—and masculine—energy in all of us. Women, men, non-binary people, we all suffer when we judge or deny this part of ourselves, and the disconnection we experience from this lack of trust throws us off balance.

Imbalances in the way we perceive our more feminine qualities or characteristics lead to dysfunction. We can see this at play in our society, where certain identities (gender, race, class, sexuality, religion, physical abilities, etc.) are more valued and therefore carry more power than others. This lopsided, inequitable system colors every aspect of our lives, from the structures we rely on (healthcare, education, housing, employment, etc.) to the way we view and value ourselves. It truly is the proverbial soup we are all swimming in. The result is quite harmful, as it disrupts the natural state of harmony seeking to exist between the feminine and masculine aspects of ourselves.

The time has come for a major shift in the way we think about the qualities of the Sacred Feminine. We must heal the places within us, individually and societally, that cause us to fear or have contempt for any part of ourselves, including the parts that are uniquely and divinely feminine. In doing so, we will begin to value the qualities of the Sacred Feminine—understanding, creativity, receptivity, tenderness, ability to flow, etc.—and the Sacred Masculine—assertiveness, strength, giving, courage, focus, etc.—equally, allowing both aspects of ourselves to work in tandem to create a healthy, balanced state of being—one that evolves beyond these two seeming polarities.

Frankly, this transformative act is required to enter childbirth and motherhood in an empowered way. Doing so not only changes you, it changes the world around you. As you begin to heal the divide within and begin to truly value the feminine qualities innate in us all, you will wake up to your goodness and remember that these are the very qualities that make you the powerful keeper of life that you are. When we take back our power and self-trust as women, the rest of the world will have no choice but to see and know us wholly.

To help understand the importance and value of what we bring to the table as women, we need to look no further than the Sacred Feminine. This subtle, yet consistent, source of creativity and life is all around us. All we need to do is to remember it and learn to recognize it.

CHAPTER 2: THE SACRED FEMININE

"Motherhood: all love begins and ends there."

— Robert Browning

The concept of a powerful feminine force that supports all of life is a staple in cultural and religious traditions around the world. This essential source of life is referred to by many names: "Sacred Feminine," "Great Feminine," "Divine Feminine." This trusted and relied upon source of feminine energy is often personified as the archetypical mother, or "the Great Mother."

In many cultures, the Great Mother encourages fertility, protects against disaster, and aids in times of trouble. Often, she exhibits numerous aspirational qualities. From the spiritual traditions of the Himalayas, Tara is the female deity of compassion. Throughout China and Southeast Asia, Guan Yin is revered for her assistance in times of adversity. In Egypt, images of mother goddesses predominated many archaeological finds. Isis, the Great Mother and protector, and Hathor, the goddess of fertility and love, dominate the walls of temples and tombs. And in ancient Greece, sanctuaries and temples were dedicated to the Great Feminine in her various forms, including Gaia, the personification of the Earth, and Athena, the embodiment of courage, creativity, and wisdom.

In Rome, the qualities of the Great Mother were found in Minerva, the goddess of wisdom, as well as Venus, the goddess of romantic love and fertility. The Sumerian goddess Inanna, a prototype for Venus associated with love, beauty, sex, war, justice and political power, is yet another image of the Great Mother. And much later, with Catholicism, the Virgin Mary became the epitome of purity and devotion as the mother of God.

As you can see, the lens through which a culture or religion views the Great Mother determines which of her qualities it celebrates. The same holds true for the many indigenous societies of the world. Because these cultures often have a close connection to the Earth, they tend to recognize and honor the female body and its keen alignment to the rhythms of nature.

The link between women's bodies and nature is perhaps most evident when we consider the moon. As the moon progresses through its phases, so does a woman's estrous cycle. This process takes about 29.5 days for the moon and 28 days for a woman's menstrual cycle.

For the Maya of ancient Mesoamerica, the sun is also associated with an important female process: pregnancy. The 260-day Tzolk'in calendar was correlated to women's gestation period and is aligned with the rhythm of the sun's waxing and waning influence over the seasons.

For the Hopi of the Southwest in North America, Mother Earth and the Corn Mother are believed to be the mothers of all living things. In this and similar traditions, the concept of the Great Mother is closely linked to the Earth and its many gifts and powers, such as life-giving waters, the sun, and the night sky.

While icons of the Great Feminine vary from tradition to tradition, she is almost always revered as a generator and caretaker of life. In fact, the qualities of these female figures are surprisingly consistent from one culture to the next. Whatever her form, she is usually seen to be a protector and guardian of life. In some cases, the framework of entire societies was structured around these qualities.

In her book *Matriarchal Societies*, Heide Göttner-Abendroth describes a wide variety of matriarchal societies spanning from Asia to the Americas, existing for hundreds of years at a time. Each culture had its own unique take on the Great Mother, but the values these societies held were based firmly in those of the Great Feminine. For example, governments were organized by consensus and equality, and economic systems were based on mutuality, generosity, and sharing.

Göttner-Abendroth also cites the Haudenosaunee people who thrived for thousands of years in the northeastern part of North America as exhibiting matriarchal values. In their society, as in other matriarchal societies, the concept of private property did not exist. Instead, they built communal buildings that every member of the community shared. Everyone had a home, and everyone had a place. Nurturing and caring for all the members of their society was a primary value. The economic system was based on generous gift giving, and goods were redistributed in giveaways to ensure everyone had equal access to resources. As a result, no one went without having their basic needs met within this system.

The societies Göttner-Abendroth describes are in sharp contrast to patriarchal societies, which tend to value competition, domination, and hierarchy. Today, the majority of the world's societies are patriarchies, and within them we find the results of some of the distorted aspects of masculine qualities, such as class systems, systemic racism, and misogyny. Healing the Sacred Masculine is part of the anecdote to these problems and worthy of deeper exploration beyond the scope of this book. However, acknowledging these wounds is part of the healing as is understanding how the values of the Great Feminine have long been without support in our culture and gone unrecognized by much of the Earth's population.

The result of systematically denying the values of the Sacred Feminine is a schism within societies and individuals. For contemporary women, this has meant focusing more on attaining masculine forms of power to survive within patriarchal structures. Turning our attention outward in this way has been at the expense of going inward—as we are called to do every month with our period. The result is a loss of awareness of the intimate connection our bodies have with nature.

In a similar way, the concepts of the Great Feminine in spiritual pursuits have also been largely lost. This separation is due to the dominance of masculine forms of divinity in many of the world's major religions and the longstanding men-only policies for clerics and other positions of power within many of these traditions.

Is it any wonder that so many of us feel estranged from our bodies and spirits? We are taught to ignore the values of the Great Feminine, which causes an internal rift. This causes us to feel lost and disconnected. The imbalance then blocks our ability to live life in a truly empowered way. This is where the power of the Great Mother can serve as a deeply healing balm.

By connecting to the power of the Great Mother, we can learn to see ourselves once more—or perhaps for the first time—through a clear lens, one free of the distortions of a patriarchal worldview. This allows us to create space in our lives for the invaluable qualities of the Sacred Feminine and to begin to recognize our own innate power and wisdom. Once we know the gifts that we bring to this world, we can move through our life with greater confidence and grace. This self-understanding is perhaps most needed as we approach initiatory moments such as childbirth. Like guideposts on life's path, initiations show us how well we are able to meet change when it comes our way. And, because each initiation affects the next, it is important for us to look at where we've been on our initiatory path so we can hold a clear vision for how we want our next initiation to go.

CHAPTER 3: INITIATIONS OF LIFE

"In giving birth to our babies, we may find that we give birth to new possibilities within ourselves."

— Myla Kabat-Zinn

We are all students of life, moving along at different stages of emotional and spiritual development. While our experiences are individualized and unique, we are all being pulled toward the path of our own evolution. The force behind this push for growth is not something outside us; rather, it is our own remarkable biology.

As women, our body's ability to procreate connects us directly to the creative power of the Earth. In nature, we can see the products of creation all around us with the budding trees, singing birds, and buzzing insects. What we may not consider, however, is that this same generative power is alive in us. Like the Earth, we have the power to give, sustain, and nurture life.

If we open to it, this natural alignment to the Earth reveals to us our true nature as creators. As human beings, we work intimately with the powers of creation that abound in our universe. Whether we know it or not, we are interacting with this energy every day as our bodies continuously move us through different phases of initiation.

The seven major initiations we must attend to as women are birth, puberty, menses, the first sexual encounter, childbirth, menopause, and death. These events are driven by our biology and serve to usher us into new ways of knowing ourselves. The emotional, spiritual, and mental shifts that accompany these biological changes are profound.

In a perfect world, we would be given a proper framework from which to comprehend the power and vulnerability at the heart of all initiatory processes. Such a framework would allow us to better understand these biological events and the effect they have on us as physical and spiritual beings. In truth, it is how we respond to the creative power that seeks to be brought to light during each initiation that determines how we engage with life. Our experience of initiations marks and defines us.

Likewise, ideally, we would also be given the tools needed to pass through these rites in a grounded and conscious way. This includes a strong connection to Earth, or her personification as the Great Mother, so that we may trust deeply and naturally in the infinite source of support she offers us. It is through our relationship with this feminine force that we are better able to understand and endure each initiation on our path, growing our confidence as we step into new versions of ourselves and into the next initiation when it inevitably comes our way.

As our biology calls us forward through initiations, we are urged to embody the wisdom and grace of the Great Mother. Her qualities of nurturance, protection, generativity, creativity, mutuality, generosity, healing, sharing, receptivity, adaptivity, inclusiveness, spaciousness, responsiveness, and the capacity to flow with change unfold within us and become our qualities. This process matures us, making it easier to respond to each new phase of our development by staying open.

When properly supported through initiations, we are able to stay close to the vulnerability required of us, allowing us to see the initiation through to its completion. The power of the initiatory moment, with all of our effort and openness as we transform, must be managed carefully and thoughtfully. Most importantly, that power must be safeguarded and dedicated back to us, the initiate (and our baby, in the case of childbirth). If this does not happen, the initiation will be disrupted and incomplete. An unsuccessful initiation can leave us feeling disempowered, confused, or even traumatized.

Adilah

A young, scared mother, Adilah was far from her family and home country of Morocco when she entered the initiation of childbirth. A language interpreter at the time, I was charged with bridging the communication gap between Adilah and the staff at the major urban teaching hospital where she was giving birth. As it turned out, my services for helping Adilah communicate would expand beyond the delivery room, into the realm of the Great Mother, who helped the young mother overcome a challenging birth experience.

The unfamiliar language and strange customs of her new country were causing Adilah a great deal of anxiety. She had little support from her husband because in her culture men are not allowed to help during birth. She also revealed to me that she had only realized she was pregnant a few months earlier, and she was upset because she had just gotten used to the idea of being pregnant and now she was giving birth.

Along with this adversity, Adilah was certain she would not be able to give birth in a hospital because none of the women in her family ever had. As she was telling me this, it hit me that she had signed the forms given to her by the intake staff without knowing what she was signing. I reviewed the forms and saw that Adilah had inadvertently given permission for medical residents (doctors-in-training) to enter the delivery room at any time. As I was explaining this to her, her contractions began to pick up. There was no medical staff around to support or comfort her.

Before long, Adilah was panicking and hyperventilating. I called the nurses, and then I silently called in the power of the Great Mother. Next, I began helping the frightened mother slow her breathing. Just as the baby's head was crowning, a crowd of male medical residents entered the room, led by a senior doctor who was speaking loudly about the laboring mother as if she were a specimen.

When she saw the men, Adilah panicked and began frantically trying to cover herself in the midst of a full-on contraction. I stepped between her and the interns and explained that in her culture, it was a sin to let a man who is not your husband see you at all, much less your vagina! Finally, a nurse arrived and strategically ushered the cadre of men out of the room. The baby came soon afterward.

At this point, with all she had gone through Adilah was absolutely hysterical. She could barely focus on her newborn son. She had given birth in a completely disempowered way, with no connection to the power of the Great Mother or to her own internal reserves of strength due to the many external circumstances she was faced with. Because she felt disregarded and disrespected by the hospital staff, she doubted her ability to keep herself and her child safe. She had no connection to the different phases of her body's development as she moved through the birth, no consistent assistance from hospital staff, and no one to help her recognize and stay connected to the larger sources of nourishment the Great Mother had to offer her.

Adilah was distraught because of the traumatic nature of the birth. A nurse came in and tried to give her a shot to calm her down, but Adilah refused. The nurse became more insistent, which made the new mother even more hysterical. I asked the nurse if I could just sit with Adilah and speak with her in her native language so that she could feel like something was familiar, suggesting that it might calm her down. The nurse agreed and took the baby for tests. I took the opportunity to do a guided meditation to help Adilah connect with the power of the Great Mother.

She was able to connect with this power through the image of her grandmother. She immediately relaxed, and I offered her some suggestion hypnosis around her ability to learn how to mother, to know her baby, and to hold on to her traditions in a strange land. After the meditation, she was calmer, and when her baby returned, she was able to welcome him with a smile. Adilah's connection to the Great Mother helped mitigate the trauma she had experienced in a situation where the power of her initiation had not been held properly for her.

Unfortunately, like Adilah, few of us are successfully guided through our initiations. The result is a disconnection, a loss of trust in ourselves and others. As our bodies force us to transition from one way of being to the next, we may question our ability to endure such change, or worse, we may resist in fear. Perhaps, with reluctance, we rely on our will to see us through. But will alone cannot help us when we are standing at the precipice of transformation. In fact, it may stall the process entirely.

Without a doubt, childbirth is one of the most life-changing initiations we can go through as women. How we approach giving birth is largely informed by the ways we have faced previous initiations. If we fight an initiation, it will be a battle. If we welcome it and try to stay open with help from the Great Mother, our experience will likely be more easeful and even empowering.

It is important to gain some awareness around our past initiations before giving birth. We need to consider our feelings about these experiences. The story of our birth, our reaction to the first spot of menses blood, whether the first sexual encounter with another felt safe and pleasurable or was something altogether different—all of these experiences leave their mark on our psyche and spirit. If left unexamined, we may be unpleasantly surprised should we come face to face with these old wounds during future initiations.

In particular, the initiation of childbirth opens us up so completely that past traumas or long-denied fears we had tried to bury may overwhelmingly rise to the surface. However, we may also discover parts of ourselves that we could not have imagined existed, such as a superhuman source of inner strength and power. In this way, the experience of giving birth is an undeniably creative process, a journey into the unknown that, as it unfolds, reveals to us who we truly are.

When the natural process of birth is allowed to take its course, we have the opportunity to come to terms with anything that arises. With proper support, we are more likely to experience a transformation, a great shift into a new way of understanding and being. However, when the birth process is interrupted or improperly managed, the power of the initiation can be lost or distorted, as we saw with Adilah.

It is not always easy to look at our history in a deeper way, but doing so will help us better understand what we need in order to step more fully into our power, even in the most difficult circumstances. If past initiations have been painful or harmful in some way, it may be helpful to work with a skilled mental health provider or spiritual counselor who can provide additional support.

CHAPTER 4: THE SEVEN INITIATORY STAGES

"We are all butterflies. Earth is our chrysalis."

— LeeAnn Taylor

The following is a list of the initiations of life for girls and women. I have paired each initiation with the qualities of the Great Mother that become available to us as we pass through each respective initiation. I have also provided exercises to help you gain a greater understanding of your own initiatory experiences. A major opportunity for growth comes when, as the initiate, we are able to recognize and integrate the lessons from each initiation and the qualities of the Great Mother into our life.

BIRTH

Birth is our first experience of the world as an individual being. The qualities of the Great Feminine emphasized in the initiation of birth are nurturance and protection.

Once we are born, we no longer exist as one with our mother's body. Instead, we begin the natural process of separation, as we move from an aquatic state of complete dependence to a world of air where we must breathe to survive. As relatively helpless beings, we require intense physical care. It is through our helplessness that we learn about nurturing, safety, and security.

Stanislov Grof, M.D., an influential transpersonal psychologist, says that our birth can serve as a template for our life. According to Grof, the experience of being born and the type of nurturing (or lack thereof) that we receive as newborns becomes the foundation for everything we experience later in life. If we are well nurtured, we carry this experience with us, and learn to care for ourselves. If we are not nurtured well, we may be fearful and harbor a sense of lack within us. In fact, it is this lack of nurturance early on that causes many of us to embark on spiritual quests in search of a feeling of wholeness.

The care we receive as infants and children determines how well we are able to trust. Our ability to trust that we will be protected is what sustains us as we move through life's most challenging moments. This trust can pierce through anything that might frighten us, allowing us to be less fearful and more fully present in the world.

The good news is, regardless of the degree of nurturance we received from our human mother, we can learn to trust in the power of the Great Mother to protect and sustain us. When we realize we can confront our fears and find protection through our willingness to trust, we begin to engage with life in an entirely new way. The nurturing that this protection provides is an essential quality of the Great Feminine, one that informs us all our lives.

Cecilia

Cecilia, a slight woman in her forties, came to my Depth Hypnosis practice seeking help. She was feeling a strong sense of guilt for not wanting to take care of her aging mother, who required in-home care for her failing health. I asked Cecilia about her relationship with her mother over the course of her lifetime, to which she responded, "I feel really guilty about this, but I have never felt close to my mother. One time I heard her talking to my aunt about the time I was born. My aunt was saying, 'Yeah, that was really awful, everything you had to go through. It was a bad time from start to finish. You threw up the whole time and then you had all those breast infections. And the birth itself… I would not wish that on anyone! And not to mention that she never slept and was always crying.' I didn't realize they were talking about me until I heard the last few words. My mother always told me how much I cried as a baby."

I asked her how these difficulties might have affected their ability to feel comfortable and close with each other. "Yeah, maybe that's why I don't feel close to her. I could see that." As we continued talking, it became quite clear how the emotional distance and lack of affection she felt from her mother at the time of her birth was echoed as Cecilia entered puberty. She needed guidance when she first got her period, but she didn't feel like she could talk to her mother about it. Instead, Cecilia struggled to get herself tampons and hid the fact that she had her period from her mother and from others.

I asked Cecilia if it was easy or challenging for her to get emotionally close to the women she dated. She admitted that it was hard for her to get close to her partners emotionally. The distance created by all of the difficulties surrounding her birth was carried forward into subsequent initiations. The circumstances of Cecilia's birth had indeed become a template for experiences later in life. I suggested that, before she could make a decision about her role in caring for her mother, it might be helpful to reclaim the power she had lost during her previous initiations. She agreed.

Over the course of the next several months, she had emotional and spiritual breakthroughs as she learned more about how her birth experience had negatively affected many areas of her life. Cecilia's birth did indeed set her on a spiritual quest through which she gained a lot of insight and understanding about the coldness she often felt toward others.

Francesca

Unlike Cecilia, Francesca had a completely different experience when she was born. She described her birth as easeful. Her parents were excited and there were no complications with the birth. She was about twenty when she came in for help with her boyfriend, Brendon, as they were having relationship difficulties

She said, "You know, I feel so guilty. Brendon is a wonderful person, but he has so many problems. He really had a tough time growing up. I don't even think his parents wanted a kid when he was born. He doesn't have any baby pictures or anything. I have all these pictures and my parents always talk about what a great baby I was. He had a really tough time in high school and had difficulty with his first girlfriend. I had a great time growing up. I really did not know that things could be so hard. I feel like there is something wrong with me that things are so easy for me."

Of course, there was absolutely nothing wrong with Francesca for having a wonderful life. In fact, hers is a good example of how a well-held birth initiation can create a solid foundation for later initiations. While she had a little insecurity in high school, she had good friends and a steady boyfriend until graduation. She felt stable and supported through her transition into puberty and she felt safe and nourished in her first sexual experience. Conversely, the disrupted nature of Brendon's birth was reflected in the rocky experiences he had in later initiations.

The Initiation of Birth

Like Cecilia and Francesca, your birth and the stories around your birth may impact you in ways you may not be aware of. Take a moment to reflect on what you've been told about your birth and write it down in a journal or notebook. You may also want to ask any relatives and friends who were close with your family when you were born what they recall about your birth and write down those stories, too. Consider how you feel about the stories you've been told about your birth or that you are learning about now. How do these stories affect your feelings about giving birth?

PUBERTY

Puberty begins the shift from childhood to adulthood. The qualities of the Great Feminine emphasized in the initiation of puberty are creativity and generativity.

The change we undergo at puberty is very clear. As children, we are incapable of reproduction, but with puberty, we can now participate in the creation of life. As we step into puberty, our childhood falls away and our journey into adulthood begins. The lessons offered to us at this time revolve around identity as we become sexually mature. Questions begin to fill our head: *Who am I now that I'm changing so much? Who was I before? Who will I become? What does it mean to be a woman? What will my parents think of me now that I'm not a little kid anymore?*

At puberty, we are trying to distinguish ourselves as an individual within and away from our family and society. We are trying to understand what our unique desires and needs are and how to express them within the context of the collective. This type of inquiry is an essential aspect of our spiritual growth. As we transition into adulthood, the initiations our bodies take us through teach us a great deal about ourselves. If we stay close to what our biology is showing us about who we are and how we express ourselves in the world, our self-knowledge deepens.

Unfortunately, this process of self-exploration is often co-opted by our society. By and large, our culture has lost touch with the importance of ancient puberty ceremonies, which are still performed in traditional societies around the world. In these practices, it is understood that there is great power in the moment when childhood is left behind and a new adult is born. Those in charge of upholding the cultural norms of the group oversee these rituals, which are designed to bind the new adult to the priorities of the collective. From that point forward, the new adult is expected to consider the needs of the group and to uphold its values.

It is important to recognize that some puberty rituals or practices from traditional cultures are painful or oppressive for the initiate, and I am not condoning the appropriation of such practices. However, there is a wide span of experience between initiatory rituals that may, for instance, require body mutilation or dangerous feats of courage or strength, and an absolute amnesia surrounding the importance of puberty for the adolescent. And although we have largely lost the ability to recognize and mark significant initiatory moments as a society, there are some traditions that still uphold the sacred nature of this biologically inspired event.

For instance, within the Jewish tradition, the puberty rites of bar mitzvah for boys and bat mitzvah for girls are still very much alive. As a child becomes an adult, they are expected to study the Holy Scriptures, master a passage of the texts, and present their accomplishments by reading this portion to the congregation. They are then celebrated as an adult member of the community who has promised to uphold the values of the tradition above all else. The bat and bar mitzvah rituals are very good examples of a ceremony that marks the moment of initiation, when the old form of the child is left behind as the young adult steps into the community of adults guided by their shared Jewish principles.

Shira

When I first met Shira she was thirteen years old and suffering from panic attacks. At the root of these attacks was a trip to Jerusalem that her family took in honor of her upcoming bat mitzvah celebration. It was supposed to be a joyous trip, which included visits to the city's many holy sites. Shira, however, had a powerful reaction to being in Jerusalem, where she felt overwhelmed by all of the history and stories of the Jewish people held in the monuments and temples there. After returning home from the trip, Shira began having panic attacks. That's when her mother contacted me and asked if I could help.

When I asked Shira what was happening for her, she replied, "I just cannot go through with this! This is all too much for me. I don't know who I am anymore. Am I a Jew? Am I Shira? Am I just going through with this because it's what my parents want for me? All the history I saw on the Israel trip was just so overwhelming. What do *I* have to do with all of this? How is this *me*? Why am I automatically a part of all this? I don't mean to be ungrateful, but I just can't handle this."

I was impressed with Shira's ability to articulate her feelings of overwhelm as she confronted this important initiation, which was designed to have her dedicate herself to preserving the ancient cultural identity of a people and a history she wasn't ready to fully embrace. I helped the family come to an agreement to postpone the bat mitzvah until Shira better understood what was happening for her. Shira felt immediately relieved. Her parents, however, were quite unhappy about the change in plans; but they were so concerned for their daughter's well-being they agreed to wait.

Fortunately for Shira, she had a high level of awareness about the issues she was grappling with. Equally fortunate (and rare) is for a cultural system to accommodate the concerns of the initiate the way Shira's congregation and parents have done. I have worked with many people who struggle to know themselves outside of their identity as members of a religious orthodoxy. This inner conflict often affects their ability to connect deeply with others, making it challenging for them to step into intimate relationships and meet the next steps in their initiatory path in a clear and grounded way. The support Shira received from her family and spiritual community enabled her to process and heal from the issues causing her panic attacks.

Kathy

When she came to see me, Kathy, a plump, dark-haired, twenty-nine-year-old woman, was in the throes of what she called "a dark night of the soul." As her thirtieth birthday loomed, Kathy felt distraught because she had assumed she would be married with children by now. The problem was she struggled to form long-lasting relationships. She also had envisioned having a more high-powered job by the time she turned thirty. Essentially, what Kathy was experiencing was a crisis of meaning, feeling as though she was not living up to her potential and that she was wasting her life.

In order to try to understand what might be contributing to her situation, Kathy and I explored her experience of early life. It turned out she was raised in a very religious household. As she became a teenager, she began questioning the second-class role that women were expected to take in her church. As she entered high school, her parents pressured her to be confirmed, but she refused. Her parents went as far as to threaten Kathy, saying they would disown her if she did not go through with confirmation. Still, she refused. They sent her away to a boarding school despite it being the middle of her freshman year, and she never really lived at home again after that.

By looking into her past in this way, Kathy was able to understand how the painful experiences in her adolescence were contributing to her current existential crisis. It was clear that her initiatory path at puberty had been severely disrupted. Her experience of the initiation of puberty was characterized by rejection. First, her church rejected her for being a female, as she witnessed through the second-class treatment that the women congregants received. Then, she was rejected by her parents for refusing to bind herself to their religion through the confirmation process. As a result, she rejected herself as a woman and as an individual.

The pattern of rejection continued as Kathy refused to enter into long-term relationships because she feared being marginalized. This made it impossible for her to have children, which was important to her. The subsequent initiations of sexuality and childbearing were interrupted by the disrupted experience of the initiation of puberty. Kathy had to do a lot of work to emerge from this crisis, most of which had to do with reclaiming the power lost during her puberty initiation. Reclaiming this power allowed her to know herself without having to reject herself or others.

The Initiation of Puberty

Your entrance into womanhood began with puberty, when the first shift in hormones caused you to experience your body in a new way. During puberty, we often become more aware of our bodies, and our perspective of ourselves also shifts. Take a moment to reflect on what you remember about this time in your life and write down your thoughts. Then, consider how you might have been affected by these early experiences, and write down those thoughts too.

MENSES

Menses occurs each month when a woman's body changes form, and her uterus builds and sheds its lining. While the physical change is evident, the emotional changes she goes through are complex and often not well understood. The qualities of the Great Feminine emphasized in the initiation of menstruation are adaptivity and receptivity.

Perhaps the biggest change that happens at puberty is when a girl gets her first period. This momentous occasion marks her ability to procreate. With the menstrual cycle, our bodies are in a constant state of ebb and flow throughout the month. This ongoing change is central to many women's experience of life. As women, our bodies require us to continuously engage in the cycle of life and death with the building of form (the thickening of the uterine lining) and the tearing down of that form (the sloughing off of the lining) each month. Through the phases of our menstrual cycle, we are directed biologically toward a deeper inquiry into the nature of change.

As part of the initiation of puberty, menstruation is closely linked to the Sacred Feminine quality of generativity. This is because in order for us to be able to generate new forms, we must accept the dissolution of old ones. If we reject change and attempt to clutch to what once was, we lose the creative potential alive within the new. Creativity and generativity, and their intimate connection with life and death, are the essence of our human experience.

In particular, as women we are called to stay open to the many births and deaths in our bodies and lives. If we're unable to make peace with the inevitability of this cycle, we may become guarded in an attempt to protect ourselves from the always-changing nature of life. When we respond to our periods in this way, big problems can arise. For instance, every month we may find ourselves in mourning over the end of our childhood and its lost freedoms that we experienced when we first got our period. Or, we may struggle to tolerate the pain that our cycle causes us. Whatever the reason, when we reject our monthly menstrual cycle, we fray the connection between our body and spirit.

As we discussed earlier, our biology is what leads us toward personal and spiritual growth. So if we have a negative response to our period, we may block the creative power that this monthly initiation offers us. We also run the risk of losing connection with our body and our ability to understand and meet its needs. When this happens, any number of emotional and mental problems can arise, from eating disorders to identity confusion. In truth, if we reject the flow of change of our monthly cycle, we can become our own worst enemies.

Zahar

Zahar, a hard-driving advertising executive in her forties, came to see me for help with anxiety, which sometimes bordered on panic. As we explored her history, I learned she was taking medication to suppress her monthly periods. When I asked her about it, she responded, "I just don't have time for periods. They are messy. They make me moody. I just cannot be bothered! It is the same thing with men. I don't want to get married. I don't want to do these women things!"

What Zahar did not yet understand—as it is not in our collective awareness—is that the hormonal shift we experience every month with our period gives us access to our deeper emotions. These emotions, which are always present, become more pronounced as our period nears, and are often dismissed as "PMS" or premenstrual syndrome. What actually occurs, however, is a vitally important aspect of the initiatory process of menstruation. This is the moment when the veil between our conscious mind and our complex emotional and mental world is lifted. This unveiling can feel inconvenient or difficult to deal with, especially if we've been trying to keep certain emotions or thoughts at arm's length. Still, it is a necessary undertaking to attend to our deeper thoughts and feelings so that we can lead happier, healthier, fuller lives. It is also another teaching from our monthly cycle about the flow of change.

When I offered this perspective to Zahar she was silent for a long time. Then, she said, "But when I have my periods, I remember the prison and the things they did to me there. If I don't have my periods, I don't think about that time." As it turns out, when she was in her early twenties, Zahar had been imprisoned by the government of a Middle Eastern country for trying to set up schools for girls. She had been tortured during her time in jail, and all of the physical pain from that experience rose to the surface whenever she felt the pain of her monthly period.

I asked Zahar if she thought the anxiety and panic might be related to her time in prison. She looked at me in surprise, "But I never think about it at all! How could it be?" I explained how our conscious mind tries to filter out painful or confusing experiences, and that these filtered experiences don't actually go away. Instead, they move into the deeper reaches of our mind and body, only to surface when the hormonal shift of our monthly cycle brings them into our awareness. I suggested to Zahar the possibility that she was re-experiencing the trauma from her time in prison as anxiety, even though she had done her best to block it out. Zahar agreed, and although she was very unsettled at the thought of working more directly with her trauma, she agreed to try. We set out on a path to help her heal from her imprisonment so that she could once again return to the natural rhythms of her body.

In Zahar's case, the experience of her monthly cycle was interrupted by trauma and her attempt to distance herself from that trauma. As a result, the initiations of sexuality and childbirth that typically follow the initiation of menstruation were also interrupted. She did not want to marry because she did not feel she could bear to be close to a man (men had been her torturers). She did not want to have a baby because it would tie her to a man.

Addressing the trauma gently and with compassion was key to Zahar's healing of the initiation of menses. While it was difficult at times, her healing journey opened new doorways of experience for her, and Zahar learned what we all learn when we follow our body's wisdom: If we align with the initiations our biology brings to us, we will continue to grow and learn about who we are.

Chelsea

Chelsea, a friend of one of my children, had a very different initiatory experience than Zahar. Chelsea's parents were hippies, and they were all about New Age ceremonies and Earth-based rituals. When she got her period at 13, Chelsea's parents held a ceremony that was attended by all of the women in their community. Each woman offered Chelsea a blessing and a wish as she stepped into her new role as a woman. As a result, Chelsea felt very supported by the ceremony and her community. Her monthly periods reminded her of this support and of her positive identity as a woman who could bring life into the world. Although she had some physical discomfort with her period, Chelsea felt as though she could take time to care for herself each month. Her mother had taught her about the traditions of the red tent in some cultures where women join each other in contemplation during their periods. Chelsea's initiation of menstruation left her feeling very much at peace with her periods, and excited for her life as an adult.

The Initiation of Menses

The first experience of menses is a significant event in a girl's life. How you responded to your first period, as well as the response of those around you, play an important role in your relationship to your body and your identity as a woman. Take a moment to reflect on what you remember about your early experience of menses. Write these memories down. Then, reflect on how you might have been affected by these early experiences, and write down these thoughts too.

SEXUALITY

The first sexual encounter requires that we shift our focus from ourselves to include another. The qualities of the Great Feminine emphasized in the initiation of sexuality are mutuality and receptivity.

The next significant change our bodies take us through is the first sexual encounter with another person. While not generally viewed as an important stepping stone on the path of human spiritual development, sex is a powerful vehicle for gaining knowledge of ourselves and others. The education that having sex offers us about learning to receive (through pleasure) and consider both our experience and another's (by meeting our partner's and our own desires) is incomparable.

Spiritually speaking, how we engage with sex determines the lessons we will take away from the experience. To meet someone sexually, we must have a healthy understanding of our own wants and needs. When we have an open relationship with ourselves in this way, we are able to stay receptive to our partner during sex. That's really what sex requires of us: to be both receptive *and* giving as we merge into a union that is designed to move us beyond the individual experience of the self. In effect, sex, when engaged consciously, allows humans to fully embody themselves and communicate sexually in order to lift each other up toward a greater awareness of consciousness.

When we know ourselves well and we know our bodies well, we are better able to maintain a strong sense of self, even as we seek to transcend the self through orgasm, which has the potential to awaken us spiritually. When we have awareness around the teachings offered to us as we express ourselves to another intimately, the act of sex can be revelatory. In fact, learning to open and connect in this way is at the heart of the subtlest forms of spiritual inquiry, and is directly accessible through our sexual life.

Unfortunately, in many cultures sex and sexuality have been commodified, making it difficult for initiates to enter into the first sexual encounter with clear eyes and open hearts. Because we are flooded with harsh and, at times, violent sexual imagery through media exposure, many of us struggle to recognize and follow our own sexual desires and impulses in a balanced way. Sadly for some, the first sexual encounter is unwelcomed, which can complicate a person's relationship to their own sexuality. To compound the problem, some religious doctrine claims that our human sexual urges are sinful, which, of course, could not be further from the truth.

This situation is a spiritual conundrum of the highest degree. All of the misguided sexual messaging flying around confuses and harms us. Awash in the culture's harmful external input, our ability to trust ourselves and even our own bodies has been disrupted, and the doors of sexual violence in its many forms have been left wide open—something I know many people have been hurt by. In this turbulent environment, the deeper power of sex is co-opted by forces alien to the expression of the Great Feminine, such as pornography, and is now virtually unrecognizable to us. However, we can take back the power of sex by reclaiming our relationship to our bodies and learning to listen to and view them as the great teachers that they are. Only then can we stay open to the power of sex and align ourselves with its greater teachings.

Joanne

Joanne, a reserved twenty-eight-year-old, learned about the power of this kind of realignment when she came to me for intimacy issues she was having with her boyfriend. As it turned out, Joanne had always struggled to enjoy sex and would find ways to dodge her partners' advances whenever they initiated sex. When she first came in to seek guidance about the problem, she didn't fully understand why she avoided sex. As we explored her history, Joanne admitted that an older brother had molested her from the time she was eight until she was twelve. She had never told anyone about this experience. As she began to investigate it further, she realized she had never wanted to have sex because of all the complicated emotions the experience with her brother brought up for her. She wanted to be able to enjoy sex with her boyfriend, but she didn't want to talk to him about the abuse.

We spent several months working to process and heal Joanne's relationship to the trauma her brother had caused her, helping her make peace with her body. The experience with the brother had completely interrupted the initiation of puberty for her. She had been in a state of emotional and sexual paralysis since that time and was therefore unable to fully meet the initiation of her sexuality. When she had done enough work to lessen the effect of the molestation, Joanne began exploring her sexuality for the first time. Within a few more months, she felt she could discuss this work with her boyfriend, which she felt was vital to her being able to fully enter into a sexual relationship with him.

Like Joanne, many women have had traumatic experiences that have left them with a sense of shame and disconnection around sexuality. Even for those who have not experienced sexual abuse, the general view of sexuality in the United States is shrouded in shame and misinformation.

Vittoria

Vittoria came to the United States from Italy to teach modern languages to high school students. When she arrived at her new school, she soon learned that all faculty members were required to teach a class outside of their expertise or to coach a sport because the school was new and not well funded. Vittoria was asked to teach sex education.

Informed by Italian culture, Vittoria viewed the first sexual encounter as a special moment during which both people must communicate clearly with each other about their hopes and expectations. "This is the most beautiful moment of a person's life! It must be celebrated!" she exclaimed in her heavily accented English. She found that many of her students, and even some of the faculty, had no idea what she was talking about.

She was distressed to learn that many of her students were having their first sexual experience against their will. Or, they were having sex only when drunk or high and therefore could not remember the experience and its effects on them, let alone use it to deepen their romantic relationships. Vittoria was appalled to learn that many of her students were learning about sex through pornography, and that their first encounters with sex were through this distorted lens.

Vittoria and I spent many afternoons in lively conversation as she expressed her shock and tried to figure out how to help her students understand the initiation of sexuality for what it is, a moment of mutual exploration and acceptance. She created a curriculum that was designed to help her students understand their choices around sexuality and help them make informed decisions about how they engaged sexually. She sought to emphasize the positive aspects of sex and taught her students how pornography did not support a mutual, positive experience. Although some of the members of her academic community found her advocacy a bit off-putting, they all agreed that the students benefited from her approach. Thanks to Vittoria, many young people received the information they needed to pass through this initiatory experience free of the confusion and powerlessness that are part of the first sexual encounter for so many.

The Initiation of Sexuality

Your first sexual encounter is a significant life event. The conditions and circumstances surrounding this event likely still impact your intimate relationships in ways you may not have imagined. Take time to reflect on your first sexual encounter. Write about it in your journal or notebook.

Then, reflect on how you might have been affected by this experience and write down these thoughts, too. You may also want to reflect on and write about other significant sexual experiences and how they have shaped your intimate relationships.

CHILDBIRTH

Childbirth requires us to expand our focus from the self to another, redefining ourselves to include the needs of our child. The qualities of the Great Feminine emphasized in the initiation of childbirth are creativity and generosity.

Childbirth is a powerful creative process that seeks to bring us into flow with the creative force at the heart of all manifestation. To be able to move through this sacred initiation successfully, we need to have a connection with this force of creation so that we are able to stay open and surrender to it fully. Also, we must honor and follow our creative instincts when giving birth. For that to happen, we must feel protected and cared for by those around us. Feeling safe and connected in these ways is what allows us to concentrate and to go inward, where we can tap into our deep reserves of strength.

Perhaps more than any other initiation, childbirth teaches us where we are on our path of personal and spiritual development, and how far we've come in our ability to face and overcome challenges. As our bodies move us through the phases of the birthing process, we will know which qualities of the Great Feminine we have mastered in past initiations and where there are still opportunities to grow.

No matter how a past initiation may have unfolded, we can gain the lesson our biology sought to teach us by learning to connect with the forces of creation at our core. Not only can we heal experiences of past initiations by aligning with this energy, we can also direct its power toward future initiations. This force is always available to us, and when we engage with it during childbirth and other creative endeavors we are brought into connection with the power of our own creativity.

It is important that every person involved, whether they be mothers-to-be,

31

partners, midwives, doulas, or other birth attendants, recognize and appreciate the vital role they play in the sacred initiation of childbirth. There is a significant amount of power that occurs when a mother enters the initiation of childbirth and her child enters the initiation of birth. For both initiations to move as smoothly and safely as possible, those assisting with the birth need to protect and actively guide this power back to the mother and child. To hold this kind of grounded birthing environment, it is helpful for birth assistants to learn to connect to and work with the power of the Great Mother, which we will discuss in detail in Chapter 7.

As we move through the process of giving birth, we learn how to nourish and protect, watch and guide, and eventually let go altogether as our child evolves beyond us. With childbirth, women enter a whole new level of learning as we become mothers and learn to nurture and protect our children and ourselves. Partners and fathers who participate in the birthing process and in the care of their children also learn these dramatic lessons. In fact, anyone who cares for others, whether stray animals, a garden, or any being in need of tending, is immersed in these teachings of the Great Feminine.

Elaine

I knew Elaine through our children's co-op. She was a ruddy-cheeked farm girl from Nebraska who did not shrink at the idea of hard work. She ran a busy household with three kids all under the age of seven and was pregnant with her fourth. Elaine's first three births were relatively straightforward and she did not expect her fourth to be any different. When the contractions started, she took time to get things squared away with her other children. She called her best friend, Kate, to come over to watch them and waited for her husband, Jason, to come home from work to take her to the hospital. Jason and Elaine had recently moved to Berkeley to be closer to Jason's new job. But Elaine chose to give birth in San Francisco at the hospital where she had delivered her other children. This sense of familiarity was important to Elaine.

Kate arrived just as Elaine was finishing cleaning up the kitchen. Kate took the kids to the park for some fresh air and to get them out from under their mom's feet. By the time Jason arrived, things had progressed rather quickly. She told him that he had better drive like the wind and hope for no traffic. They got in the car and headed over the Bay Bridge when it became clear they were not going to make it. Elaine ordered Jason to pull the car over and call 911. Jason jumped in the backseat with Elaine and assisted her in bringing their daughter, Anna, into the world. Not long after the baby was delivered, the EMTs arrived and took over.

Both Jason and Elaine tell the story of Anna's entry into the world with a great deal of mirth. When people ask if Elaine was scared, she said that there was no time for fear. She and Jason had been through this three times before and they just did what they instinctively knew how to do. The birth of Anna is a beautiful example of how important trust is when giving birth. Because Jason had been by her side for all of her births and was there holding the space and providing her with exactly what she needed, Elaine was able to flow with the unexpected circumstances of her daughter's birth. Her trust in her partner and his ability to hold her made all the difference in what could have been a very frightening experience.

Mary Anne
Mary Anne, a free-spirited friend of mine, learned firsthand about the importance of protecting and preserving the creative force of birth when she was working on a small dairy farm in New Zealand. Early one morning, she was awakened when she heard shouting coming from the milking barn. As she struggled to put on her jacket, hurried footsteps pounded past her cabin. She followed the farmer and his son to the barn, where they found a big Black Angus laboring in the early morning light. The cow was having difficulty and was doing her best to get comfortable, getting up one minute and lying down the next. The farmer's wife, Lorna, had both her hands and arms inside the cow. "There are two babies here!" she shouted. Her son replied, "She will never be able to give birth to them both. We are going to have to put her down!" "No!" his mother shot back.

Lorna then began calling out instructions, telling everyone what she needed to help the cow give birth. Helpers dispersed in all directions to get Lorna what she needed. Mary Anne was up near the cow's head, speaking softly to her. Lorna, temple veins bulging, reached all the way up the cow's birth canal and pulled out a wet calf. Just then, the veterinarian arrived. As she took over for Lorna, Lorna turned to her son and scolded, "I never want to hear you give up on a mother like that again! Your job is to support our mothers, not throw in the towel on them!"

Mary Anne's story is an excellent reminder of the importance of those who support mothers and babies as they make their way through their initiations. It requires dedication to protect and preserve the creative power of another's initiatory experience in this sacred way. As you will see in Chapter 8, when the birthing environment is infused with the Great Mother, the initiates are supported in very real and substantive ways. You can help strengthen this support by calling in the power of the Great Mother and directing it toward the mother and child.

The Initiation of Childbirth
Whether you have experienced the initiation of childbirth or have been a witness or assistant to another's, the experience of giving birth or being present for a birth is powerful. If you have given birth, take a moment to reflect on the experience and circumstances of each time you gave birth, noting the ways you felt supported or unsupported in your journal or notebook. If you have not given birth, reflect on the significant births you have been part of, or the stories you have been told about birth. Then, consider how you have been affected by your direct experience or knowledge of these experiences, and write down your conclusions.

MENOPAUSE

Menopause requires us to redefine ourselves as we lose the capacity to reproduce. The qualities of the Great Feminine emphasized in the initiation of menopause are adaptability and the capacity to flow with change.

Menopause marks the stage of life when we are no longer able to give birth. Most people think menopause is something only women go through, but, in reality, men lose their ability to procreate too, which is often experienced as "erectile dysfunction." This initiation, and the meaning we extract from it, is central to the way we define ourselves as we get older. If we are able to meet this initiation with an open heart, we will see it for what it is: another biologically-driven opportunity to look more closely at how we view ourselves and our place in the world.

As initiations go, menopause is most akin to puberty, as menopause requires us to contemplate how we relate to the rest of society and how society defines and relates to us. It is not uncommon for older women and men to feel as though they are somehow less valuable once the creative potential of their biology has shifted with menopause. It doesn't help that many cultures reinforce this idea. This is certainly true in the United States.

In stark contrast, some traditional societies have women step into positions of power once they have passed through menopause. For instance, among the Haudenosaunee, the Native Americans of the eastern seaboard of North America, it is the highly respected grandmothers, or *gantowisas,* who have always managed the economic, social, and spiritual requirements of the society. It is worth noting the main ceremonies *gantowisas* oversee revolve around mutual benefit and gift giving, both important qualities of the Great Feminine. Through regular feasts and ceremonies, these respected elder women manage the redistribution of goods to ensure that no member goes without food or other necessities.

What societies like the Haudenosaunee understand about a woman's entry into menopause is that the massive creative power of a woman's body in her reproductive years is now concentrated within her and is no longer being diverted toward the enterprise of procreation. It is understood that this power can be a great source of wisdom and creativity from which the entire community can draw upon.

The initiation of menopause is crucial because it offers us the opportunity to identify and illuminate the lessons we have learned on our journey through life thus far. By turning inward, we can focus our energy on cultivating powerful inner gifts, such as mystic vision and clairvoyance, as well as learn to alchemize difficult past experiences into wisdom. It takes patience and skill to cultivate these qualities, especially after a lifetime of looking externally to define who we are and what our role is in society. Yet once again, our biology, forever the faithful teacher, shifts with the initiation of menopause and invites us inward, so we may discover the power and gifts of our very own spirit.

In our youth-obsessed culture, it is not surprising that so many people resist moving into this later stage of life. As we begin to lose our identity of youthful vigor, we may struggle to reconcile the process of getting older with our youthful image of ourselves. Whether we embrace our move into elderhood or resist, it will impact the quality of our lives. Resisting it could prevent us from fully harvesting the wisdom of our experience and the depth and joy that it brings us.

Naomi

At fifty, Naomi was exceedingly distressed by her graying hair and aging skin. While I tried to help her understand that her judgments about herself were creating her suffering, she would not hear it. To erase the lines in her face, she began a monthly regime of Botox injections. She also had her hair dyed every five weeks like clockwork. As soon as her periods began to wane, Naomi started hormone therapy. Then, we lost touch for about five years.

When I saw her again, Naomi's face was red and puffy from the injections and her eyelids fell heavily, drooping sideways. She was wearing a thick mask of make-up, and rarely removed her big dark glasses. When she spoke, Naomi was a bit manic, stating rapidly how wonderful everything was. I wondered if the change in her demeanor had anything to do with the hormone treatments. It was difficult to see Naomi this way, knowing that her avoidance of the aging process had created so much imbalance inside her.

Angela

A third-grade teacher for over 35 years, Angela, a spry woman in her early seventies, had been forced into early retirement because of her age. She admitted that her transition into retirement had been shaky, leaving her feeling anxious, and fretting over things she really didn't care about. Then, one day she heard about a shelter for mothers and children that was looking for kitchen volunteers. She decided to go help out. Once Angela arrived at the shelter, it was clear that many of the children were behind in their schoolwork, and some struggled with basic reading skills. In no time, Angela had started a reading program at the shelter, which she supplied with discarded books from the school where she had taught. To her delight, Angela was spending most of her days teaching children how to read again. She also became a beloved mother figure to the mothers at the shelter who were having trouble making their lives fit together. To her credit, Angela made choices that allowed her to share her wisdom, born of many years of experience, with the generations that followed her.

When we enter menopause, we have the opportunity to begin to turn years of life experience into wisdom that we can then share to help younger generations, just as Angela did. In fact, there are thousands of women from around the globe and all walks of life who are doing just that with the International Council of Thirteen Indigenous Grandmothers. An international alliance of indigenous female elders, the Council focuses on issues such as the environment, internationalism, and human rights. Council members, elder women from Nepal, Brazil, Gabon, Mexico, and many other countries, come together every six months to offer their wisdom to those who come to their gatherings. Through their example, these elders are showing younger women the importance of moving gracefully into this stage of life so that the creative potential of age is not lost.

When we understand the creativity at the core of the initiatory process of aging, we can look inward with confidence and glean the wisdom from our lives, which we may impart for the benefit of others. Then, we can prepare to receive the teachings of the last and least understood of our biological initiations—death.

The Initiation of Menopause

While menopause is an unlikely place for women preparing for birth to be focused, it is an important initiation with opportunities to gain wisdom and power as we mature. It can be helpful to consider this future initiation as it relates to the context of our lives. One day you will enter menopause and no longer be able to bear children. Will you resist like Naomi or embrace your new role in the world like Angela? Take some time to reflect on your ideas about menopause and growing older, writing down your observations. Do you have judgments about it? Do you fear or resist it? Then, reflect on several of the important women in your life who have reached this stage in their lives. Write down your impressions of them and their contributions to you and to others. If you are reading this book and have already entered menopause, reflect on your experience of entering menopause and how it met with or did not meet with your expectations of this time of life.

DEATH

Death takes us into the mystery beyond life. At the moment of death, we step away from the guidance of our body and rely on our spirit. Our ability to receive guidance from our spirit depends on how well we have followed the path toward spiritual development that our body has laid out for us. The qualities of the Great Feminine emphasized in the initiation of death are responsiveness and spaciousness.

Death is the least understood and most feared of life's initiations. Due to the great mystery of what happens after we die, many of us try to avoid thinking about death at all. Yet others of us seem to spend our whole lives in search of what lies beyond the moment we are released from our carnal teacher, the body. Regardless of where we fall on that spectrum, death is an initiation that we will all walk through one day. How we meet this initiation depends on our ability to stay open, to surrender to the vast spaciousness of the unknown, just as we have been asked to do by our bodies with every single initiation leading up to death. As with prior initiations, our relationship to the Great Feminine and her powerful, unwavering support is what will sustain us as we move through the final initiatory process of our life.

The initiation of death is important because it is the culmination of all our other initiations. How we have met, or struggled to meet, the initiations that our biology has offered us throughout our life will have a direct effect on our ability to engage successfully with the process of dying. As I write this, I imagine many readers reflexively cringing at the thought of their own death. This is not surprising since our culture encourages us to avoid thinking about death at all costs. In fact, we are guided by the fears of our culture to look away from aging people altogether because they remind us of our own mortality. This kind of head-in-the-sand approach to life's initiations, especially the initiation of death, leaves us ill-prepared to handle this biological event that, if we have been paying attention, our body has been trying to prepare us for our entire life.

Alternatively, in Buddhist teachings there is an awareness of death that is fundamental to the spiritual practice. Buddhists are encouraged to accept and even cultivate an attitude of surrender to the experience of life. This is designed to prepare those engaged with the process to stay open to the mystery that lies beyond life. This idea is found in the expression: "To live a good life, live your life with death on your left shoulder."

The vast majority of us fear our own death, just as we have feared the changes our bodies have taken us through as we have moved through life's initiations. If we struggled as we entered puberty, we may also find ourselves struggling with the initiations of motherhood. If we haven't made peace with our monthly periods by the time menopause arrives, we may suffer as our definition of ourselves changes and the creative force of our reproductive capacity moves inward. There are numerous personal and cultural reasons why many of us have constricted in response to our biological initiations. No matter how we moved through past initiations, we have the opportunity now to recognize the fact that these events are designed to strengthen our awareness of our bodies and deepen our spirits, to teach us to open our hearts and heal so that we feel supported and empowered when we are facing death.

Joseph

For four years, I worked as a volunteer in the hospice ward of a large convalescent hospital. I had the good fortune of assisting many people as they entered the initiation of death. What stood out to me was how everyone had a unique relationship to the fact that they were dying. A man whom I supported named Joseph was convinced he had been placed on the wrong ward. He had been a soldier most of his life and had a strict military regimen of exercise and self-grooming that he adhered to daily, even as his strength began to fade.

I had the privilege of sitting with Joseph as he was actively dying. Even then, he was in denial about the situation. He tried to keep everything in an orderly fashion around him, making sure his glass of water on the table next to his bed was exactly where it should be. Just as he was losing consciousness, he reached for what he thought was his glass of water and brought it to his lips to drink—but it was the call button for the nurse. He was immediately enraged that he hadn't managed the action of drinking water properly. He threw the call button to the floor, cursing himself under his breath. I felt so sorry for him that his last conscious act was to condemn himself for not being able to stand in defiance of death. Joseph was ill equipped to surrender into the unknown of this next phase of experience, his own death, because surrendering was not something he felt he could do during his life. He died resisting, which made for a difficult and uncomfortable passage. Unfortunately, Joseph was not aware of the receptivity and spaciousness of the Great Feminine, and was deprived the support she could have provided him as he went through his final initiation.

Giulia

A 92-year-old Italian woman named Giulia had no fear of death. She was a devout Catholic who had attended mass almost every day of her life. She had a special relationship with the Virgin Mary, which she was quick to tell me about when she came into my office at her granddaughter's request.

Giulia had just learned that she had a fast-growing, inoperable brain tumor. Her granddaughter was convinced that Giulia wasn't grasping the severity of the diagnosis because she was so calm when she received the results of her medical report. Giulia's granddaughter wanted me to speak with her in Italian to make sure that she understood, and then she wanted me to do some counseling work with the two of them so Giulia could come to terms with her impending death.

As it turned out, Giulia had already come to terms with her death. She completely understood and accepted her situation. Her granddaughter, who was distraught, kept insisting that her grandmother must not understand that she was going to die in a few short months. Giulia turned to her beloved granddaughter and said, "Cara, I am not afraid. I have lost and gained so many things in this life. I lost my home to the war. I lost my husband to the war. I had your beautiful mother. I have the blessing of you in my life. These are all part of my life. Madonna (the Virgin Mary) has been with me every step of the way. She was there when I came to this country. She will be with me when I leave it."

Giulia had spent a lifetime cultivating acceptance and spaciousness with the support of her spiritual practice. The Virgin Mary is, of course, the embodiment of the Great Mother in the Catholic religion. Giulia's relationship with the essence of the Great Feminine through Mary had supported her through all of the challenges and initiatory moments of her life, allowing her to surrender to them. For her, it was natural that this same support would be there for her as she surrendered to this final initiatory process.

The Initiation of Death

The final initiation of death is one that is not often considered in the West, but is perhaps the most important of all. As we saw with Joseph and Giulia, how we live our life greatly impacts the way we die. How will you prepare for the initiation of death? Have you ever considered this before? Take some time to reflect on your ideas about death and write down your observations. Then, reflect on several of the important people in your life whose deaths you attended or that directly affected you and write down your thoughts.

Further Thoughts on Initiation

It is truly remarkable how our biology is always moving us toward greater maturity and self-understanding. Through our seven key initiations, from birth to death, our bodies are inviting us to look at the places where we need to grow so that we may open up and fully embody the experience of being alive. As we have seen in the stories shared in this chapter, those who deny or suppress their experience struggle through their initiations—and likely future initiations—and those who are able to embrace the changes their bodies take them through are able to pass with more ease through these major initiatory events.

In doing the exercises above, perhaps you discovered where you have grown as the result of your own well-held initiations. Or, maybe you have noted some areas where healing is needed. Whatever you have learned by looking at your own initiations, know that this knowledge will help you prepare for the initiation of childbirth and other successive initiations. Once again, this is where the Great Mother becomes an invaluable support. In Chapter 7, you will learn how to connect with this powerful presence so that you can feel supported in all of life's initiations.

CHAPTER 5: THE MEDICALIZATION OF BIRTH

"In our every deliberation, we must consider the impact of our decisions on the next seven generations."

— Haudenosaunee maxim

As we learned in the previous chapter, how we experience our biological initiations affects us greatly. Sometimes our own fears block our ability to open and surrender to the initiatory process. Other times, forces outside us make it difficult to stay close to the wisdom of our bodies and flow with its many signs and signals. While necessary medical assistance saves lives and prevents all manner of tragedies, it is important to understand the ways in which the initiation of childbirth can be disrupted by a default approach to medical intervention. To better understand the current state of childbirth so that we can make well-informed decisions about how we want our initiation to unfold, it helps to look at the roots and progression of the medicalization of childbirth.

For centuries in Europe, female family members, friends, and neighbors were the main support system for birthing women. These chosen birth attendants often had years of collective personal and hands-on childbirth experience among them. While there was no formal midwifery training program until the seventeenth century, those drawn to the role apprenticed with advanced midwives to learn the skills needed for effectively assisting a laboring woman and her baby before, during, and after birth.

It was in the Middle Ages in Europe when men began to take an interest in childbirth. At the time, barbers—men primarily charged with cutting, trimming, and shaving men's hair and faces—also performed surgical procedures. Reluctantly, midwives would call upon barber-surgeons when birthing women were in grave danger. In time, barber-surgeons came to view birth as a profitable enterprise and began to monopolize the process. Furthermore, it was at this time in history when women from all walks of life were being labeled as witches. Midwives were among the many targeted, and they were exiled, punished, or even burned at the stake.

By the 1700s in England, the Anglican Church wielded considerable power, including over childbirth. Church fathers were charged with issuing licenses to those who were permitted to attend births, which had a negative effect on the practice of midwifery. It is worth noting that the predominant view held by church fathers at the time was that women were being punished with labor pains for the original sin of Eve, who, according to a story in the Christian Bible, disobeyed God by eating an apple from a forbidden tree.

This bias against women persisted in the English colonies. By the early 1900s in America, it was clear that birth had become a business and the men in charge of granting licenses to midwives were government bureaucrats rather than clergy. To ensure their success, many leaders in the medical community began instituting policies that encouraged women to only see doctors in hospitals, virtually abandoning home births and the midwives who typically oversaw them. The campaign against the age-old profession of midwifery was in full swing by 1915, with influential doctors Joseph DeLee leading the pack.

In a widely published text by Dr. DeLee, he states that birth is a pathological process requiring intervention from medical doctors. By 1930, the American Board of Obstetrics and Gynecology (ABOG) had been established. The Board lobbied Congress to exclude all nonmembers from attending births. With this victory, the ABOG was able to exclude midwives from the delivery room altogether. The greater effect, however, was that almost no women were present at births, since at that time most medical schools admitted only men. This discriminatory push toward male-dominated birthing environments set the course for the medicalization of childbirth that we see today in the United States.

In 1937, 37 percent of all births in the U.S. occurred in hospitals. By 2010, that number had increased to 99 percent. Coincidentally, by 2010, 32.8 percent of childbirths in hospitals were Cesarean sections. This is more than double the rate the World Health Organization recommends for Cesarean births, which it suggests should not exceed 15 percent of total deliveries in any country.

Certainly, science and medicine are important adjuncts to the birthing process when needed. Many lives have been saved by modern medical procedures when insurmountable obstacles have arisen during childbirth. However, the tools of medicine should not supersede the natural process of giving birth. When it comes to childbirth, medical interventions are best used in moderation and with great consideration, not as a matter of course.

In her book *Pushed*, award-winning investigative journalist Jennifer Block offers an excellent example of the way our culture has come to regard medical interventions as the norm for childbirth rather than the exception, and how intervention is not necessarily the better choice for healthy mothers and babies. In her example, an unintended experiment occurred at Florida Hospital Heartland Medical Center (now AdventHealth Sebring) in Port Charlotte, Florida, when Hurricane Charley struck in August 2004.

The entire city lost power for nearly a week, which forced the hospital to step away from its standard procedures for labor and delivery. Under these circumstances, births in the hospital largely occurred without drugs or medical intervention. Specifically, all inductions were cancelled and Pitocin, a drug given to induce labor, was not administered. Epidurals also were not administered. Doctors did not break a birthing mother's amniotic sac or "water" to speed up the birth, and pregnant women who came to the hospital not yet in active labor were sent home. Notably, almost no Cesarean sections were performed.

Normally, all of these procedures are routine in hospitals around the country. Epidurals are given for pain. The water is broken, and Pitocin is administered to begin or speed up labor. Cesarean sections are commonly recommended not only when the life of the baby or mother is at risk, but also when labor is taking longer than is common or convenient.

Block's findings are truly impressive. As a consequence of the hospital's necessary shift away from the standardized medical treatment of birth, fetal distress and interventions after birth dropped to almost zero. Even first-time mothers had relatively quick and easy labors. Most interestingly, the births that occurred at Florida Heartland Medical Center during the days-long power outage were more evenly distributed between day and night, as compared to the usual concentration of births at the hospital, which occur during "working hours," or Monday through Friday between 9 a.m. and 5 p.m.

While there are no simple solutions for transforming the current medical system into one that is more attuned to the natural rhythms of birth, it is nonetheless an important conversation to have. At the very least, it is essential that we begin as a culture to recognize the fact that childbirth is not a medical procedure like setting a bone or removing an appendix. Rather, it is something much greater with far-reaching effects. Because the current medical approach is to assist only on the physical level, women are left unsupported emotionally, mentally, and spiritually during childbirth. To add to this vulnerability, we have largely lost touch with the traditions that once connected us to our ancestors and the Earth and that anchored us so that we were able to navigate the transformative nature of birth more effectively.

Over the last forty years, some important inroads have been made to reduce the medicalization of birth. This includes an increase in midwifery and doula training programs, as well as the establishment of birth centers that provide an "in-between" option for women who do not want to give birth at home or in a hospital. The result is an increase in out-of-hospital births, with home births rising by 77 percent from 2004 to 2017 and birth center births more than doubling.

We also are seeing an increased demand for birth support professionals, such as midwives, doulas, counselors, acupuncturists, chiropractors, hypnotherapists, and massage therapists, as women become more aware of the significance of birth as an initiatory event and its implications for personal development. Likewise, around the world women are filling prenatal yoga classes and workshops as they prepare their minds, bodies, and spirits for the sacred initiation of childbirth.

As our knowledge of the entire birthing process grows and we comprehend its effects on us physically, mentally, emotionally, and spiritually, we can have more agency over the way we give birth. As we take ownership of our experience, we will feel more empowered and better able to hold onto the power of birth that belongs to us. In doing so, we can channel that power into a greater connection with our own evolution, the growth of our children, and the healing of the planet through the creation of a more conscious society.

The idea of connecting to a power greater than ourselves for support and guidance isn't new. It is common to most cultures, ancient and contemporary. In many traditions, we are required to give up our power and relate to this higher source of power in a specific way. While this is helpful for many people, it can also be disempowering. This is why connecting to the Great Mother is not prescribed and is personal and unique to each individual. When we connect to the power of the Great Mother in our own way, it is actually a way of stepping more fully into our personal power, which is integral to giving birth from an empowered place and protecting the integrity of our initiations.

As we will see in Chapter 6, no matter where a birth happens—at home, in a birthing center, or in a hospital—having a strong connection to the Great Mother throughout the process infuses it with the power, grace, and protection needed to support the laboring mother and her child completely.

CHAPTER 6: RECLAIMING THE INITIATION OF CHILDBIRTH

"Birth is the epicenter of women's power. "

— Ani DiFranco

Modern women are faced with an inordinate amount of pressure when preparing to give birth. Because the culture we live in does not value the greater spiritual relevance of childbirth, the people and systems set up to assist us during the process can quickly disrupt the natural unfurling of this sacred initiation. Due to our collective and individual ignorance about the gravity of initiations like childbirth, we end up inadvertently giving our power away to others.

Insurance and pharmaceutical companies, hospitals, and uninformed doctors and medical personnel can play a role in co-opting the power of the initiation of childbirth. Even friends and family members can siphon the power of this grand initiatory event by projecting their fears and experiences onto us. All of these influences make it difficult to feel empowered when making decisions about childbirth and, more importantly, during the birth itself.

As we discussed in Chapter 3, one stunted initiatory experience tends to lead to others. Incomplete initiations make it exceedingly challenging to heed the call of our biology to grow and develop as spiritual beings, to embrace each new version of ourselves as we strive to engage wholly with our life. Based on the level of interruption from unnecessary interventions in many births today, it seems reasonable to suggest that a lot of women are undergoing incomplete initiations when giving birth. The result is a spiritual crisis that can leave us feeling confused, lost, and extremely disempowered. While not often understood, an unsuccessful childbirth initiation can be linked to the common mood disorder "postpartum depression." A disrupted birthing experience can have long-lasting repercussions and impede our ability to step fully into our new identity as a mother.

The lack of information regarding the significance of childbirth as an initiatory process affects more than birthing mothers. Without a proper understanding, ministers, teachers, doctors, and other birth professionals charged with guiding women through birth are unable to provide the level of care needed once the initiation is underway. Partners also miss out on their own deeper experience of the initiation of birth when they are uninformed.

The good news is, we can help change all this by remembering the spiritual component at the heart of our initiations and vowing to ourselves to enter the sacred initiation of childbirth with a well-informed mind and a deeply connected heart. In doing so, we take back our power, allowing us to move through the initiation with greater clarity, strength, and ease. From our own education, we can teach those around us about the deeper meaning of the initiation of childbirth.

In recent decades, midwives and other birth professionals have been working hard to spark dialogue around the reclamation of childbirth. Ina May Gaskin, an early innovator of the modern midwifery movement has been called "the mother of authentic midwifery" for her part in moving the conversation forward. In 1971, Gaskin and her husband Stephen established one of the first non-hospital birthing centers in the U.S., known as "The Farm." The Farm Midwifery Center, in Lewis County, Tennessee, emphasizes the spiritual significance of childbirth and recognizes the importance of having family and friends present at the birth. The Farm is still an active birthing center today. Throughout her long career, Gaskin has received many awards for her work in the field of midwifery, written several influential books, and taught workshops throughout the world.

The American Journal of Public Health published a study about The Farm in Tennessee, tracking outcomes of care received there by 1,707 women between 1971 and 1989. The births at the birthing center were compared with over 14,000 physician-attended hospital births in 1980. The author of the study concluded: "Based on rates of perinatal death, of low five-minute Apgar scores, of a composite index of labor complications, and of use of assisted delivery, the results suggest that, under certain circumstances, home births attended by lay midwives can be accomplished as safely as, and with less intervention than, physician-attended hospital deliveries." As is so often the case, the study shows what nature knows: healthy women are fully capable of having safe births without unneeded medical interventions, particularly when presiding birth attendants are educated about and value the spiritual aspects of childbirth and create birthing environments informed by this awareness.

Despite the gains made by the modern midwifery movement, the conversation around birth remains one-sided much of the time, with medicalized birth as the dominant practice. But as women and birthing professionals seek out new possibilities for deepening the experience of childbirth, they are bringing the conversation back to the basics of birthing—be it at home or in a hospital. As women regain a foothold in the birthing world, the experience of childbirth will be transformed from a medical procedure to its original form as a biological initiation designed to connect us with our power and creativity. I saw the power of this wisdom firsthand in a birth I attended as a language interpreter.

Esther

A young Haitian woman, Esther, had come to the hospital with several women from her community. She wanted them to be in the delivery room with her, but the admitting staff would not allow so many people into the room where she was to give birth, as it was against hospital policy.

When she realized she could not have her community members by her side, Esther became tense and agitated. Her labor stopped progressing at about five centimeters. She became very upset as the nurses tried to hook up a Pitocin drip in an effort to bring the labor on again. Esther spoke French and Creole, and I was called to the birth to interpret in French and English.

As her labor became more complicated, Esther could only speak in Creole. I was able to understand about 80 percent of what she was saying, as Creole and French are quite similar.

At one point, she began crying out, pleading for her friends who were in the waiting room. She kept saying, "They will know what to do! They have the songs!" I kept interpreting as best as I could, although I thought I was probably misinterpreting the word "song" as it did not seem to make any sense. There was one nurse who was a bit more open than the others, and I stepped out of my professional role as an interpreter and begged her to allow the friends to come in. She had just begun her shift and could see that she was going to have a lot on her hands with this birth if she didn't allow the friends into the room, so she got permission for them to attend the birth.

The nurse asked me to invite in Esther's friends. I found the members of her community in the waiting room, sitting quietly, focusing deeply, and humming softly together. It seemed as though they had been waiting for me, as they simply got up and walked toward the room before I could say anything. They hummed softly as they entered the delivery room. Esther relaxed immediately. As I closed the door, they began clapping softly and started singing in rounds. The energy in the room became very alive. Esther sang with them, and soon her labor picked back up. She gave birth within several hours, with her support network singing around her.

After the birth, I asked the women what songs they had been singing. Adele, a tall, bright-eyed woman, told me they were the songs that all the women in their village sing for each other during labor. "These are the songs that our grandmothers sang at our own births and they are the songs we sing for the new generations," she said. She also told me these songs were often sung at special ceremonies, such as those held to commemorate a girl when she gets her first period.

In his acclaimed book, *Beyond the Brain*, Stanislav Grof, M.D. suggests that a woman's own birth serves as the template for how she will approach childbirth. After witnessing Esther's experience, I reflected on Grof's words and realized how much she needed to hear those songs that were sung for her when she was being born so that she could give birth in a way that felt good to her. The songs connected Esther to the other times in her life

50

when, during previous initiations, her body moved her through pivotal moments of change. She needed that deep connection to traverse the initiation of childbirth successfully, and when she feared she could not have the songs and the energy and comfort they provided her when she was being born, Esther began to lose her focus and courage.

It was as if the songs held the power of initiation within them, transmitting that power from one initiation to the next. For Esther, they seemed to connect her to something very deep and subtle from her own initiation of birth and of puberty. The power contained within the songs enabled her to give birth in a way that connected her to a long unbroken line on the initiatory path she was a part of. If she had not been allowed to connect with the power of the songs, the initiatory moment of her child's birth likely would have been incomplete. Esther would have lost power if she had been forced to receive the Pitocin, rather than the power of her songs. In turn, she would have lost control over the entire birthing process. Instead, she was able to direct the power the songs provided her toward her own well-being and the well-being of her child. Through their singing, Esther and her friends connected to the Great Mother, allowing Esther to give birth in an unhindered, empowered way.

CHAPTER 7: CONNECTING TO THE GREAT MOTHER

"You carry Mother Earth within you. She is not outside of you. Mother Earth is not just your environment. In that insight of inter-being, it is possible to have real communication with the Earth, which is the highest form of prayer."

— Thich Nhat Hanh

Like Esther, I first encountered the Great Mother during a challenging birth experience in which I almost died. Appearing as a bright, compassionate presence, she sustained me at my greatest time of need. Even though the birth lasted more than 24 hours, I never took my focus off of the Great Mother and her loving, supportive presence.

This unwavering force of life-sustaining power is available to us all. Whether she appears to you in a vision, rides in on the notes of a sacred song, or another scenario entirely, the Great Mother will guide and protect you in the way that best supports you.

There is perhaps no greater time of need for a woman to call on the Great Mother than when she is giving birth. That is why I created the Great Mother Meditation, a tool designed to help women as they move through the initiation of childbirth. The meditation is a subtle yet powerful way to connect with the power of the Great Mother, a power that resides within you, and to work with it in the modern birthing environment. Partners, midwives, and other birth attendants are also encouraged to use the meditation so they too can connect with the power of the Great Mother as they support women and babies through the birthing process.

Cultivating a connection with this powerful, vital force allows us to invoke the Great Mother with confidence and to fortify our efforts to safeguard the power of the initiation. Whether we are the birthing mother or a birth assistant, learning to "call in" the power of the Great Mother is an important part of the process and an element common to most initiation rituals. In the Great Mother Meditation, it is the Great Mother who helps you access your power and guides the initiation of birth.

Many cultures have a tradition of calling upon this trusted feminine force to protect women as they birth their children. In ancient Japan, the Mother Goddess Tamayorihime was believed to help guide the birthing process, and was celebrated for her role in childbirth through Shinto rituals. The Mother Goddess of ancient Greece, Hera, presided over all births, assisting women as they labored. And Ajysyt, the Great Mother of the Yakut people of Siberia, was said to oversee every birth, aiding the mother and carrying the soul of the child.

But we don't have to obey any culturally defined rules or hold any set of religious beliefs to encounter the Great Mother. She may be perceived in any form that has meaning to us. In fact, how we perceive her will vary depending on our needs. For instance, one birthing woman may see her as soft and loving, while another sees her as fierce and driving. She may come to us as a fairy, and to our friend she is a bear. However the Great Mother appears to you, know that her power and teachings are meant to nourish you as you give birth and to sustain you in the moments when you need her most.

The simplicity of the Great Mother Meditation ensures that all birthing women and their support team members are able to encounter the Great Mother easily and on their own terms. It doesn't even require that you believe in a power called the Great Mother or believe in a higher power at all. It just requires an open mind and a willingness to give it a try. Then, you can decide for yourself what you have experienced. Even if you decide it is your imagination, the imagination is a powerful force.

Based on my work with visualization therapies, traditional hypnosis, Depth Hypnosis, and certain shamanic principles, the Great Mother Meditation is similar to a hypnotic induction and is extremely effective at connecting birthing women and their caretakers to the power of the Great Mother. In fact, it is helpful if both the birthing mother and those planning to assist her follow this meditation before the actual birth. Doing so develops trust in the Great Mother and your experience of her, as you connect with her repeatedly over time. Ideally, birthing mothers who encounter the Great Mother through this meditation will connect with her again and again throughout pregnancy and childbirth for guidance and nourishment.

Similarly, if the care team can connect regularly with the Great Mother before the birth, it will help them connect more deeply to their own power and inner guidance. It will also help them increase their trust in the supportive, powerful force of the Great Mother and improve their ability to guide and protect the lives of the birthing woman and her child as they make their way through their respective initiations. Those charged with supporting the birthing process can create a remarkably effective energetic safety net to ground the experience when they connect to the power of the Great Mother as a collective.

There are a number of ways for a pregnant woman to enter the altered state of awareness where she will meet the Great Mother. One way is to have a trusted person, preferably someone who has worked with the Great Mother before, guide her inward with the Great Mother Meditation. Another way is to have a caregiver who has not worked with the Great Mother yet who is willing to support the birthing woman by guiding her through the meditation. Finally, a woman may connect on her own to the Great Mother before and during birth by recording herself reading this meditation and listening back to it. You'll find the Great Mother Meditation in the back of this book. You can also find a recording of this meditation at sacredstream.org.

It is quite a magical moment when we connect, or when the person we are assisting connects, to the power of the Great Mother for the first time. To rest in this connection and feel the limitless compassionate energy of this force as it moves around or through us is an experience we won't soon forget. More importantly, it is the beginning of what may become an incredibly supportive, life-affirming relationship.

The following accounts are drawn from my students' experiences, as they have learned how to work with the Great Mother Meditation. They are all professionals from a variety of backgrounds who work with women in various stages of birthing. In some cases, they have helped their clients or patients connect with the Great Mother. In others, they themselves have experienced the healing presence of the Great Mother.

These excerpts were taken from the moment in the meditation described in the last chapter when the person first encounters the Great Mother. As you will see, each person meets the Great Mother in their own unique way and develops their own personal relationship with this power. There is no right or wrong way to connect with this energy. However the meeting unfolds is exactly as it should be.

ↁ

"She is the creative force and ground for all of life..."

I ask to meet the Great Mother. I am standing in an open place. A great wind blows toward and around and over and under me. I feel very afraid of this power. It is huge, and full of light and sound and torrential movement. I am close to being knocked over. My guide stands behind me. He braces me and helps me to move forward toward the source of this energy. With him, I find my courage. It takes Herculean effort to move forward into the streaming wind and movement. I lean in, and I move forward slowly. Finally, I am able to jump into the center, into the source of the wind. The Great Mother appears in white. She says, "You have passed the test. You are now to be my handmaiden." She is beyond good and evil. She is more powerful than all. She encompasses all. She is the creative force and ground for all of life. She takes me to her garden, and we sit and have tea.

ↁ

"She shows me the spirit of my son..."

I am standing by a mountain. There is water running, and grass. It is sunshiny. Beautiful. Calm and warm. I am met by a butterfly. She is the Great Mother, carefree and innocent. She shows me the spirit of my son. He is heavy, and more serious. I am to sit and stay with him.

55

☙

"The Great Mother has no boundary..."

The Great Mother appears as a monolithic female Buddha. She is made of stone. She is a symbol, a door to a greater energy and the energy coming through. I am told this is a good place for me to sit each day. I am not to think here. There is a transfer of energy behind and inside the statue. It is connected to me. My instruction is to respect the connection in order to be in the right place to have this child. The Great Mother has no boundary. She is like a big ball, giving birth to herself. She is in a constant state of giving birth again and again. The transition to motherhood from here is not so shocking, it is already happening all the time. It is effortless and all connected.

☙

"I must not have resistance..."

There is a big ceremony coming. I am to give myself over while not surrendering myself entirely. There is a baby boy. He needs my physical energy to be ready. He is very joyful, and not worried. He has a plan. I am shown we have done this together before. I must not have resistance. I must not think about or judge what is happening. The Great Mother is showing me the people who will be involved in the birth. I am to thank them for participating, and to create a psychic birth plan with them. I am to get ready mentally. Then, I am to let go and be restful.

☙

"She is safe and powerful..."

I am moving up the knoll of a hill. There is a temple behind me. It is grassy all around. The temple is fuzzy. The temple turns into a brown bear on a wooden structure. The brown bear is the Great Mother. She is safe and powerful. I feel calm, protected. She roars. I can access her power. It is the birth energy. I know how to move it through my body.

☙

"Trust and faith are where I am to focus..."

The Great Mother says to be patient and not to worry. Trust I will learn how to do things. Rely on the people around me. Don't forget I'm not alone. Trusting. This is my big learning. I can look to the baby for signals about what she needs. Trust and faith are where I am to focus. It is my path. Doubt and fear bring me to my child self where I am small and disappointed. I could not talk with my mother. She wasn't really there. I sit with the Great Mother and this child part of myself. She needs a mom who is sober and present, and who will talk with her. She needs a mom who will be curious about her. As she sits with the Great Mother, I feel my child self healing.

☙

"She is the mother I never had..."

I am in a garden. There are tons of flowers. There is a white fence and a white house. There is an older woman. She is an energy, an angel, a woman. She tends the garden. She is the mother I never had. She is grounded and supportive. She says, "I'm here for you." She has such a wise energy. I always hoped someone would be like this with me. All my unsettled places are no big deal for her. She can be there and be grounded, without judgment or feeling uncomfortable.

☙

"I feel full of energy..."

I see green. There are walls and a wood floor. There are two windows. I am in a tree house. I can see branches outside the windows. I feel safe. There is a breeze. I sense it is the Great Mother. There is a giggling, and a quiet rustling of the breeze in the trees. It is the Great Mother. She is overwhelming, open, and free. I want to breathe her in. Refreshing. My heart and gut don't feel constricted any more. I feel full of energy. I can jump and dance. This is an anger-free, frustration-free place. I want to show my son this place. I can play here. Whatever I need, I can just take a deep breath in. The windows don't close. I always have access to her. Even from inside, I can still hear her. When I breathe, I picture leaves rustling in my lungs. I don't feel the constriction now. I haven't felt a presence like this in a long time.

☙

"It is a window into my baby..."

The Great Mother shines a light on me. It is a window into my baby. The baby is bigger, squirmy, and moving around. Exploring its home. The Great Mother says, "The hurt is necessary, and we will both get through it." I am to remember, whatever happens, that I am moving toward the feeling of holding my baby in my arms.

☙

"She wants me to feel love..."

The Great Mother wraps me in a love blanket. She wants me to feel love, from the heart, towards myself. It feels green…new…living. I can be the source of that. I have felt cold and dead inside. I do have the strength to do these things. I can be powerful and strong and shine this light. It's worth it, even if it is just for me.

☙

"I feel many flickers around me..."

The Great Mother is the sun. She is shining rays of light and there are nutrients pouring into me. She has laid a bed in my womb. I feel full and supple and maternal. I am told I am a part of this field of life. I am not outside looking in. I feel many flickers around me. They are spirits wanting to come in and be born.

☙

"I can again hum and shine my light..."

The Great Mother is holding me, and I hold my womb with my loving heart and my strong belly. I gave the strength in me I had to give. I'm connected to the whole life force, and I have that to share and show other beings how to plug into it. I show them by humming and having faith in my intention. I shine the light from my heart and give them (the embryos) faith and intention. They want to be part of it, my heart. My only obstacle is my fear of the things I have no control over. This grip of fear looks like something that can prevent these lives from growing. The fear can cut me off from the warmth of the love I send them. The Great Mother says, "See fear for what it is. Be compassionate towards it." This is less scary. The fear is now more like a friend who has been hurt. I can again hum and shine my light.

ᕀᔆ

"I am letting go…"

The Great Mother and other guides walk me up a hill to a very old place. There are rocks around. We go up to the top of the hill. There is a pool there. I sit. They want me to drop my hopes and wishes for a baby into the pool. I see the baby resting there safe and cared for by the guides. There is mutual care happening. It is full of meaning. I feel complete. There are lots of other pools. I'm not at the center. I am to trust that wherever I end up, it is a place where I can be. I am letting go. Opening.

ᕀᔆ

"I am to let go of the struggle…"

The Great Mother says to let go of my tightness. All is okay. All three of us are okay. I am to let go of the struggle against discomfort and not being able to sleep. I am to accept the rest I get. I am to let go of the struggle. It's quieter. I am to work with the Great Mother in labor. She will help with fear of the unknown and fear of pain. I am to let her hold my hand and open to the scary place.

ᕀᔆ

"I see myself being born…"

The Great Mother takes me to the room where I was born. I see it was full of my mother's burdens. It is difficult, but I am able to lean into the Great Mother and get the support I need. Although it is difficult to be with them, when I see the burdens in this way, I can see they are not mine. They belong to my mother. I see myself being born. As I am being born, half of the burdens in the room go away. I feel heaviness in my chest. I want to both avoid and release my connection with these burdens. The Great Mother comes, and I feel my breath full and easy as she brings warmth and light into the room and bathes me in it. It feels like the Great Mother is repatterning my connection to my mother's burdens.

ᕀᔆ

"I encounter a field of energy that I hold as I am working…"

I am in the midst of doing a healing for a client who has been working on pre-verbal trauma associated with a difficult birth and subsequent adoption.

I encounter a field of energy that I hold as I am working. There is a sound to it, a song of clucking and clicking noises. I begin to articulate these sounds as I hold the power of the field for my client. Then, an earthy female being the color of dark rich soil appears in my mind's eye. I do not have to ask, it is Gaia, the Divine Feminine, who has come to heal her beloved child.

CHAPTER 8: BIRTH STORIES WITH THE GREAT MOTHER

"Childbirth is more admirable than conquest, more amazing than self-defense, and as courageous as either one."

— Gloria Steinem

To call upon the Great Mother is to invite into your life something that is true and ever present. The following stories are a window into the initiation of childbirth when supported by the power of the Great Mother. These unique birth experiences, shared by my students when working with clients, demonstrate the benefit of being empowered when giving birth, and how connecting with the power of the Great Mother makes this possible. You will see the sometimes subtle, sometimes not, yet always miraculous ways that the Great Mother provides just the right kind of assistance. Whether this great force of life is sustaining a frightened mother through a challenging labor or breathing energy back into an exhausted woman faced with the growing possibility of a Caesarean section, the Great Mother brings about positive shifts in the birthing environment that benefit women and children as they move through this sacred rite of passage.

Remember, even if we have no spiritual practice at all, the Great Mother is always here for us with her consistent and unwaveringly supportive presence. Whether you are giving birth in a hospital, birthing center, or at home, and whether childbirth aligns with your birthing plan or goes into unscripted territory, know that you can call on the power of the Great Mother for assistance. She will never leave your side. Her power is your power and lives inside of you.

An Ancient Wisdom

From the first moment I met my client Lisa, she had a sense of calm about her. Whenever we talked about birth, a serene knowing smile would stretch across her face. She prepared for her birth by attending classes, and she had a solid partnership with her husband. She had also worked for the Peace Corps in Africa and had witnessed several births. I guided her through the Great Mother Meditation at our last meeting together before her birth. The Great Mother appeared to her as a wise, ancient African woman.

Lisa's birth was quiet. She was internally focused. Her husband and I "held space" for her. When we transferred to the hospital, the staff was very respectful of her process. She was standing in her personal power in a strong way. The birth was serene, and she was immoveable in her focus. After a couple of hours of pushing, her baby arrived. Lisa's all-knowing smile was intact as she kissed the top of her baby's head.

At the postnatal visit a few weeks later, I asked Lisa about her internal experience of her labor. She said quite simply that the entire time she was in labor she was following the steady, knowing, ancient feet of the Great Mother down a flight of clay stairs. Those stairs led her to her baby.

Pay Attention

It was late May and the flowers outside the doctor's office were in full bloom. I was excited that my pregnancy was almost over and that my baby was going to be here soon. I had come for what I thought would be a routine 36-week checkup. My doctor greeted me breezily and started to examine me. She kept moving from side to side checking me and adjusting the equipment. I thought it was a bit odd, but I was not concerned. And then the doctor started moving a bit too fast. "I just need to get a second opinion here." she said. Shortly, her colleague arrived and checked me. He immediately moved into fast gear, saying, "We have to get down to OR for an emergency C-section." Everyone started moving really fast around me and I kept asking what was going on. My doctor said, "Let me tell you on the way down to the OR. You have all the papers signed, right?" Papers? I could not remember anything that I had signed. "I guess," I said. She told the office manager to check the paperwork as we headed out the door, me in a wheelchair and trying to text my husband.

As we were going down the corridors, I could barely understand my doctor. There was something about the baby's heartbeat. I started hyperventilating and everything started whirling around me. Doors opened and closed. The lights seemed to be flashing on the ceiling. Then my husband called. I could barely talk or focus. As he realized what was happening, he almost shouted, "Listen to me! Remember the Great Mother! Remember how she came to you in the meditation we did at Isa's office last week. She said she would watch over you no matter what was happening. Tune into that now! Pay attention! I will be there as soon as I can!" It was like he was giving orders to a bunch of his cadets at the military school where he taught. He was definitely not soothing and reassuring. But it was what I needed. I started to snap out of the woozy place.

I focused back on the experience of being in Isa's office and the tingling feeling I had in my neck and arms as I felt the Great Mother reassuring me. I was put on a gurney. My doctor said, "You are going to be okay." It was almost like the Great Mother was speaking to me. I felt like I could breathe a little more easily. I just stayed focused on the tingling feeling and the sound of the Great Mother's voice as they placed a mask over my face. I am so grateful for all the work everyone at the hospital did to make sure my baby was born okay. And I am especially grateful to the Great Mother who helped me in ways no one else could that day.

Meeting the Great Mother with a Partner
My client Ana had a little scare at week 27 of her pregnancy. She was having frequent surges and she was beginning to efface and dilate. She had to go to the hospital and take medication to slow down the process, and was put on bed rest for 10 weeks.

We had our last prenatal meeting at around 37 weeks to help Ana and her husband prepare for the birth. She had met with her doctor the day before, and was told that she no longer needed to be on bed rest. In our Depth Hypnosis session, we talked about recognizing the way energy flows toward birth. I told her that sometimes when women are put on bed rest, there can be a slowing or freezing of that flow. When I mentioned this to Ana, a look of recognition came across her face. She knew exactly what I was talking about.

Ana envisioned a beautiful meadow that was covered in ice and snow. Independently, her husband also ended up in a meadow. However, in his vision, it was a beautiful spring day. He felt the sun strongly on his face. When Ana spoke, she asked the Great Mother for a healing. As the healing progressed, she saw all the snow and ice in the meadow melting. At the end of the healing, she was standing in the same meadow as her husband, with the sun on her face.

After the meditation, she reported feeling as though she had released a lot of the tension from the weeks of bed rest. Both Ana and her husband felt very close after having shared a similar vision. I got a call from them a few hours later. Ana had gone into labor and their baby was born not too long afterwards. In fact, the baby was born in the caul, or amniotic sac, which is very rare and is viewed in many cultures as an auspicious beginning for the baby.

Trusting the Process

I did a great deal of work to prepare for the birth of my child. Being an older mother just past forty, it had not been easy to become pregnant, so when we found out that I was pregnant, my husband and I were overjoyed. Complicating things was my Crohn's diagnosis. I had spent many years getting this disease under control, but stress can cause complications so we were cautious throughout the pregnancy.

Everything had gone very well until my water broke at 26 weeks and I was admitted to the hospital where I was to remain for the duration of my pregnancy. I was terrified. The chances of the baby surviving were low. Every day was a fight for the life of my baby. And every day we won that fight, we had to wake up the next day and do it all over again. I just needed to get my baby as far along as I could so that he would have a fighting chance. Then the miracle of modern medicine could work its magic.

I was fortunate to have a strong team of support to help coach me through this terrifying time. Every day I connected with the Great Mother and with the spirit of the little one inside of me. The Great Mother showed me that the baby was fine and working in his own time. She showed me my body and how it was strong and she also showed me all the places where I needed to face the fear and doubt I held.

All of these doubts about my age, my health, and my ability to be a good mother had planted seeds in me that I needed to clear in order to give birth to this child. I was shown how I needed to do my part and then give myself over to the process of the birth when it arrived. I needed to trust that the baby would come at the time that was right for him.

It was hard, but I did the work and allowed the Great Mother to guide me every morning in meditation. Some days were easier than others, but I felt her there with me in the hospital holding me as I went through this. Then at 31 weeks I went into labor naturally, and safely gave birth to a healthy three and three quarter pound baby. He went to the Neo-Natal Intensive Care Unit (NICU) where he thrived under the care of the great doctors and nurses there. And I continued to connect with the power of the Great Mother to help sustain me through the difficult weeks ahead. Today, my son is a happy and healthy first grader.

Calling on the Power of the Great Mother

My client Cindy had a prolonged pushing stage in her labor. The doctors were beginning to get concerned about the baby's heart rate. It wasn't an emergency yet, but the baby's heartbeat was definitely taking longer to recover. What was so striking about this birth is that I kept feeling as though there was a nurse behind me. Several times I turned around to speak to the nurse and no one was there. I just kept getting the sense of a very loving and nurturing angelic woman behind me. I realized that I was feeling the presence of the power of the Great Mother assisting me as I helped Cindy.

When it became clear to Cindy that her baby needed to be born, she started to chant, "Nature Mama, come on Mama," over and over again as a way to connect with the power of the Great Mother. She needed this chanting to give her the power to birth her baby, which she experienced as moving into and through her. She gathered this power and pushed her baby out. It was absolutely astounding to see the shift in the progression of the labor once she started chanting and calling for the power of the Great Mother.

Overcoming Fear

Jenny had a history of panic attacks, which is why she came to see me for Depth Hypnosis. She had been anxious about her birth, which got worse when the doctors told her they wanted to induce labor. To help calm Jenny, I guided her through the Great Mother Meditation, where she had a powerful vision of the face of the Great Mother. When I arrived at the birth, I expected Jenny to be anxious. However, what I witnessed was a very calm birthing mother. Once she sensed I was in the room, she opened her eyes. As the next surge started, she said, "Every time I have a surge, I see the face of the Great Mother. I haven't told anyone that yet because they'll think I'm nuts." Then, another surge came. The labor continued for hours, and Jenny remained calm and focused.

At one point she began to feel scared and asked for medication to ease the pain. I knew that a natural childbirth had been her goal, so I led her back to her breath and suggested that she connect with the Great Mother. I kept bringing her back into connection with the Great Mother's face that she had experienced in her first encounter with the Great Mother. Each time, I reminded her to connect to the face of the Great Mother, and each time she pulled out of her fear as she made that connection. This went on for hours.

Finally, Jenny's baby was born, without the panic attack she feared, and she had a natural birth, just as she had wanted.

Dreaming of the Great Mother
I guided Ashley and Jon, an expectant couple, through the Great Mother Meditation. They both had a strong meditation practice already. The night after I had introduced them to the meditation on the Great Mother, Jon had a dream. The Great Mother came to him as a strong and loving wise older woman. She told him that the birth would be hard, but that everything would be okay and that Ashley could do it.

The birth was lovely. They had done a lot of work to create a comforting space with calm lighting, an altar, and devotional music. The labor was going well, and then Ashley began to lose steam. She started doubting herself. We gave her a lot of reassurance, but it didn't seem to be helping. Then, Jon said, "Remember my dream and what the Great Mother said? It's hard, but she knows you can do it." This reminder helped Ashley immensely. The Great Mother's message filled her with endurance and confidence. It was as if her whole body remembered the dream and responded with renewed vigor. Shortly after, their baby was born.

Advice from the Great Mother
Lola had been laboring for close to 48 hours during her home birth. It was clear from the surge pattern of her contractions that the baby was in a unique position, which was likely contributing to the long labor.

She was getting tired, so I suggested that she get into the tub so she could relax. I knew this would be a good place for Lola to reconnect with the Great Mother with my help. I led her through the meditation and she connected with the Great Mother as she rested in the tub. As Lola meditated, the Great Mother reminded her that she has scoliosis, and it was the scoliosis that was contributing to the issue with the baby's position. She suggested that instead of curling around the baby during labor, Lola should be more upright to give the baby more space. The Great Mother suggested that I help to support her in being upright.

So I got behind Lola as she was sitting and gently aligned her shoulders, pulling a bit to help straighten her back. We did this for a short while, and everything shifted. Lola moved into active labor, and had her baby several hours later. I never would have connected the issue with the baby's position to scoliosis, and was very grateful for the Great Mother's guidance.

Listening to the Great Mother

Eve had been in labor for three days—most of that time at home. When we did eventually go to the hospital, she was placed in a room that had a birthing tub. Because of the slow onset and waning momentum of the labor, Eve was exhausted. When it came time for her to push, she didn't feel she had enough strength to be able to do it. I suggested that she take a break and try again once she'd had a good rest. The doctors were being conservative and didn't want her to wait for the delivery of the baby. They didn't like how long the labor was taking, even though the baby seemed fine. The doctors finally suggested a Cesarean. Eve became very upset.

This was one of those moments where a choice had to be made between the natural pacing of the mother and baby and what the hospital staff wanted. This can be a hard place to navigate. I suggested that Eve get in the tub so I could help her connect to the Great Mother through guided meditation. She was able to relax and connect with the Great Mother, who came to her as an image of a large woman, as big as nature with outstretched loving arms. The Great Mother told her that she and the baby just needed more time.

As she was in the tub and connecting with the Great Mother, Eve got a lot of good rest. Her strength was returning and the forces within her began to get stronger. She was able to move through the rest of the birth at her own pace and in a powerful way. Her healthy baby was born naturally. Eve had listened to the advice of the Great Mother and made the choice that was right for her, in spite of the pressure she was receiving from hospital staff to do something different.

Web of Light

Chloe labored in her home for several days. At around 3 a.m. on the third day, she announced that she wanted to go to the hospital. She realized that she was having trouble letting go at home because she felt scared. Several years earlier, Chloe had had heart surgery. She wanted to be at the hospital to have her heart monitored. Although she was still in early labor, we went to the hospital so she could feel safe and supported.

When we got to the hospital, she was checked to see how fully she had dilated and she was about four centimeters. Several hours later, they checked her again and nothing had changed. At this point, the doctors suggested augmenting Chloe's labor with medication if her dilation did not increase within the next few hours.

Chloe had described herself as "not spiritual," so I was hesitant to introduce the concept of the Great Mother to her. Instead, I connected with the Great Mother through meditation as I sat behind Chloe, who was sitting on a yoga ball and resting her head on the bed. In my meditation, I saw a beautiful and supportive energetic web of light around the laboring mother. It was in an egg-like shape around her body.

The egg expanded and then I heard, "This is seven centimeters." I realized the Great Mother was showing me energetically what being opened to seven centimeters is like for a woman during labor. So, I helped focus this information energetically toward Chloe, as I stayed focused on the Great Mother. Chloe shifted her position a bit, and I realized she was receiving this information as she rested. Her labor shifted, and it seemed that she had opened to the Great Mother's instruction without realizing that was what she was doing.

As her labor progressed, she continued to dilate. The doctors came in a bit later and checked her. Chloe was seven centimeters, and there was no more talk of giving her medication to speed up her labor. This was an astonishing and confirming experience for me. I understood the power of the Great Mother in a whole new way.

Play Ball!

My client, Sharon, comes from a big Irish family, and everyone was really excited that the first grandchild was on its way. Her father-in-law, John, was particularly excited, but he was a little worried because the due date was the day of the big game between his alma mater and their biggest rival – something he didn't want to miss! Watching these football games was a favorite family event so going into labor on the day of the big game was not ideal for Sharon or the rest of her family. As a birthing coach, I had spent a lot of time with Sharon and her husband, James, helping them prepare for the birth of their child. When I arrived, Sharon was trying to focus on the meditation I had given them to help her connect with the Great Mother. John soon arrived exclaiming, "Game day!" to no one in particular. "Yes, game day," I thought to myself. "But we are thinking about two different games."

As the labor progressed, we went to the birthing center. John decided to come with us. When we arrived, he turned the game on the TV. This was all a bit much. My client's labor started slowing down. Her husband and John were talking about the different players. My client wasn't saying anything and seemed okay with what was happening. But when my client's labor came to a stop, I made the call and said, "Okay, boys, you are out of here!" Sharon looked relieved and became even happier when I sat down next to her and began reciting the script of the Great Mother Meditation. This helped her focus inward again, and she was able to connect with the Great Mother who told her that the only thing she had to focus on at that moment was birthing her baby. As she regained her focus, the contractions started again. It turned out to be a relatively quick birth, and now she has a little girl who loves playing ball with her granddad.

The Great Mother Arises

Melissa had been laboring well at her home birth. But when the baby's head crowned, it ceased coming forward. Instead, it was crowning for about 30 minutes, which is a very long time for this stage of labor. Melissa was quite tired, as she had been laboring for a long time. The baby's heartbeat started to decelerate. The baby had to be born.

Melissa began pushing with all her might. The midwife started to feel as though it was becoming an urgent situation and expressed this to Melissa. She said, "Okay, if you don't push the baby out with this push, I am going to have to cut an episiotomy." I reminded Melissa about the Great Mother, and told her to call on her for strength. The midwives heard me, and, spontaneously, we all started calling on the power and strength of the Great Mother. We were suddenly all chanting together, "Great Mother! Great Mother!"

The power of the Great Mother could be felt tangibly in the room. It was almost as though a stream of energy flowed in from the chanting. Melissa pushed one more time, and the baby's head was born with that push. She did not need an episiotomy. She did not even tear as the baby was born.

East Meets West

Amy came to see me for acupuncture because she wanted to get pregnant. She had stopped taking birth control pills a year before, but her period had never returned. She was afraid of needles, but had several friends who had worked with me and who had become pregnant. She was willing to give it a try even though she remained skeptical.

In her first session, we just talked about acupuncture. In our second session, I was able to use three needles. We had to count them as we put them in and we had to count them as we took them out. Since Amy had such trepidation of needles, we did a great deal of visualization work. I worked by calling the power of the Great Mother into my sessions with her. My office was filled with the essence of the Great Mother as we worked. I talked to Amy about the Great Mother Meditation and one day she was ready to try it. She connected with a strong, powerful guide almost immediately. She named this guide "Abby."

Amy began working with Abby daily. Abby became her most trusted guide. As she worked with Abby, Amy became more and more connected to her own power and clarity. As this occurred, she made choices that best suited her fertility journey. She received an intrauterine insemination and she received it in a conscious way. She asked the Great Mother to accompany her on the path the insemination would create for her. As we worked together, Amy opened more and more, and she eventually became pregnant with twins. Even before she received the results, she knew she was pregnant. She also knew she would be having twins and that they were a boy and a girl. At this point, she had worked with guidance and the Great Mother so closely that she could trust her knowing.

Once her pregnancy was confirmed, she had some anxiety and fear. We worked together to ask the Great Mother to protect the babies' spirits. As Amy worked with her in this way, she became more and more clear about what each baby needed. Amy perceived that each one was protected in its own "sack" by their own guidance and the Great Mother.

Amy received acupuncture and journeyed to the Great Mother throughout her pregnancy. Toward the end of her pregnancy, she started having preterm labor. We did more acupuncture and we journeyed to the Great Mother. At the birth, I called on the power of the Great Mother to bring ease and grace to everyone. I asked the Great Mother to guide and protect this birth, and she did. We did acupuncture and visualization throughout the labor. During the entire day of labor no one came into the room to interrupt us, even though we were in a hospital.

When Amy's dilation was at 10 centimeters, Amy was feeling "done." She was exhausted. Her doctor was a perinatologist who was used to high-risk emergency births that usually involved Cesarean sections. He ordered an epidural because it was twins, and because he wanted her to have the drug in case she had to go to surgery.

Labor slowed, as it often does after an epidural, and Amy was able to rest a bit. Then, an hour later, under the watchful eye of her doctor, Amy birthed Jack, an adorable, healthy baby boy. Fifteen minutes later, out came Hazel, a happy, healthy baby girl. Amy and her husband were filled with love and gratitude to see their babies. I was grateful to the power of the Great Mother. I believe it was she who allowed the doctor to let the birth happen naturally. Interestingly, the doctor, who had been in practice for years, had never attended a vaginal birth of twins.

In the Field of the Great Mother

My sister, Michelle, had planned a home birth. She invited my partner and I to be at the birth with her husband, the midwife, and the midwife's assistant. She had a birthing tub prepared and we had worked together prior to the birth practicing the Great Mother Meditation. Her husband, Tim, and the midwife had also practiced connecting to the Great Mother in preparation for the baby.

This was my sister's second birth. She was excited about the arrival of this child, and when the due date approached, she began doing what she could to help it along – eating spicy foods and taking long walks.

I lived just around the corner from my sister at the time and when my partner, Anya, and I got the call that the birth had started, I told Anya that we had plenty of time to get over there, since things were just getting started and the labor could go all night. About half an hour later Tim called and said that we needed to get over there – it was going quickly.

We rushed over and when we entered the house, I fully expected to hear the groans of labor, but it was silent. Tim brought us upstairs to where Michelle was in the tub. The feeling in the room was serene. Within about forty minutes, the baby was born. Tim was in the tub with Michelle and caught the baby, who was born in the caul. The entire process took just a little over two hours. After my sister spent time holding the baby, she took a shower and then began instructing us on clean up. She looked great and had so much energy, it was hard to believe she had just given birth.

I had been present for two births before this one, both of them in hospital settings. This home birth was different for a number of reasons, but what I found most striking was how accessible the field of the Great Mother was and how palpable it had been for all of us. It was like the whole house was held in a protective energy that resonated within each one of us. We were all aligned and there was hardly any need to speak as the process unfolded naturally with each of us focused on the mother and her needs. It was as if the Great Mother was directing this birth and we were just actors playing our parts.

CHAPTER 9: CLOSING THOUGHTS

"The Earth is our Mother."

— Paiute chant

The human body is remarkably effective at guiding us toward the answers to those age-old questions that all religious and spiritual traditions seek to explain. *What is life and who creates it? What is the meaning of life? What generates and sustains life? What is death? What do we need to know about the cycle of life and death, and how does it affect us personally and as a collective?*

The journey our biology takes us on not only shapes our experience of the physical world; it also leads us toward a greater mystery. Through our initiations, answers are slowly revealed to questions humans have been pondering for thousands of years, to the mystery of who we are and why we exist. Once we realize our body is a key that opens the door to our spiritual self, we can begin to comprehend the significance of our initiations and how our experience of them has helped or hindered us on our path toward spiritual development.

In traditional societies, the deeper, spiritual meaning behind initiatory moments is revered as a vital force. Each biological transition, from birth to death, is honored with rituals, ceremonies, or processes designed to assign spiritual meaning to the initiations. This meaning becomes the basis for how initiates define themselves and how others define them. Because of the value systems in traditional societies, the power of initiations tends to be captured for the benefit of the group, rather than preserved and directed to the initiates themselves—not ideal for bolstering the personal power of an initiate. At the same time, the rituals and ceremonies themselves do create a coherency that does not exist in a culture like our own.

In modern societies, our rites of passage have become almost entirely incoherent. As we become more estranged from our bodies and their needs, and as we continue to lose awareness of our biology's connection to the Earth, we struggle not just through our initiations, but also through our lives. During puberty, young adults lose their way easily and, unguided, misdirect their power into a culture based in consumption and addiction. The spiritual paths their changing bodies are opening to them go largely unrecognized as teens increasingly learn about sex through pornography, which demeans and disempowers them.

Many women have become strangers to their monthly cycles, taking drugs to suppress their periods, or ignoring the cues that their emotions are trying to reveal to them during this time. Childbirth has become medicalized for the convenience of members of the healthcare system, which captures the power of birth and dedicates it to the wealth of medical and pharmaceutical companies. Menopause is feared and misunderstood as a loss of creative potency, rather than a refocusing of that power inward. And death, the great initiation into the unknown, is rejected in fear, leaving those approaching their final initiation with few resources or guidance.

Although our modern world does not recognize or value the initiations of our lives, these initiations are happening regardless, and will continue to be important markers in our physical, emotional, and spiritual development. How we react to these initiations determines the direction of our spiritual path. When we feel congruent with these physical changes, we are content spiritually. But when our reactions to these changes are heightened or out of synch, we are being shown the places where we have work to do, so that we may become at peace with who we are.

No matter the type of society we live in, the power of the Great Mother has been and forever remains available to us. Her power is the power of the Earth and, because our bodies are of the Earth, we have this power within us too. As our biology propels us forward on our spiritual path, we are shown exactly where we need to place our attention in order to mature. Our job in this process is to stay open during the initiatory moments of our lives, recognizing them as the guideposts of learning and growth that they are, and to move without constriction from one way of being to another. This is the magic we see unfolding freely in nature. When we recognize our own connection to the Earth's cycles of change, our lives take on new meaning and depth and our ability to flow with the unknown grows.

Regardless of the relationship we have had with our bodies and our initiations up to this point, we can learn now to respect and love our bodies for the consummate teachers they are and heal from the disempowering initiatory moments of the past. In fact, we must embark on this journey if we are going to be able to approach future initiations—ours, our children's, and others'—in a conscious and empowered way. First, however, we must recognize the split between our mind, body, and spirit, and how it causes us to struggle needlessly.

Nowhere is the effect of this split more evident than when unneeded medical procedures are given in the initiation of childbirth, preventing mothers and children from moving through their initiations in an uninterrupted way. When we understand our lives as a path of initiation and learn how to protect these moments of great vulnerability on our path, our priorities begin to shift. We understand that it is our responsibility to safeguard the power of our own initiatory moments as well as others'. This provides an entirely new lens through which we can view and understand our human experience.

The time has come for those of us living in modern cultures to reclaim the power of the initiatory path and dedicate it to discovering the mystery at the heart of our existence. This path is open to all of us at any time. However, it is in the birthing environment where we come into contact with one of the most potent and recognizable portals to this path. As we encounter the tremendous creativity at the core of childbirth, we begin to see the aspects of the Great Feminine that are revealed to us during the initiatory moments of our lives. We learn that the power of these initiations is our birthright. When we embrace this wisdom, we can step into a new way of being, physically, mentally, emotionally, and spiritually. By aligning with the nurturance and creativity of the Great Mother, we can meet any challenge that arises with courage and grace.

At first glance, my quest to help women understand the significance of their own initiations, especially childbirth, and to affirm their right to the power of their own initiatory processes may seem idealistic. Nonetheless, as women, it is imperative that we heal the relationship to ourselves and work with the power of the Great Mother to restore communication between our bodies and our spirits. We can reconcile the confusion and brokenness that is the signature of our modern time and learn to trust ourselves again. When we do, we will *open* to the moments in our lives when we are called to expand into our tremendous creative potential, materially and spiritually. In short, we will change the world.

I bow to the Earth and dedicate myself to her.

THE GREAT MOTHER MEDITATION

You find yourself getting comfortable. Noticing all the places where the surface beneath you meets the different parts of your body. And as you feel yourself supported in this way, notice where your breath is. Notice where your breath goes as you breathe in, and where your breath goes as you breathe out.

As you breathe in deeply and breathe out, notice how your breath is like a bridge between your outer world and your inner world, with each breath drawing you nearer and nearer to your inner world.

We are taking a journey into that place within you where everything that you have ever known or felt or sensed or imagined is recorded. And we are taking a journey to this place within you to connect with the power of the Great Mother. This may be sensed in a variety of ways. You may hear it, you may see it, you may feel it, you may smell it, or you may just be aware of it through your sixth sense, that part of you that senses things naturally.

Open to this idea in whatever way feels best to you. You may experience this part of yourself as an image, a beautiful light, a sound, as a teacher in human or plant or animal form, as an angelic or mythical being, or some other form that has special meaning to you.

But for now, just return to your breath. And as you do, just sense or feel or imagine that there is a sense of relaxation all around you. Now on your next breath, draw this relaxation into your head and face, letting all of the muscles around your eyes and jaw release any tension you might be holding. Notice your neck and throat and feel that relaxation flow down into your shoulders and into your arms and hands. Feel your fingertips as the relaxing feeling reaches them. They may even begin to tingle a bit.

Now allow this feeling of relaxation to flow down into your chest and belly. Just notice how your organs of respiration, digestion, reproduction, and elimination are bathed in this relaxation. Just feeling that same relaxation flow down into your hips, your knees, down into your ankles and into your feet. You may feel your toes tingling a bit as that relaxation reaches all the way down into them.

On your next breath try to sense or feel or imagine that this relaxation has created a star or a sun or a ball of warm light at the base of your skull. Now, sense or feel or imagine that it is radiating throughout your mind, harmonizing your brain waves and relaxing your mind. And just notice how as your mind relaxes, your body relaxes, and as your body relaxes, your mind relaxes even more. Allow yourself to sense the connection between your mind and your body as this relaxation flows slowly down your spine.

Now just feel this relaxation as it flows all the way down the back of your body. You may even feel that you are so filled with this relaxation that it is coming out of the pores of your body and surrounding you in a cocoon or cloud of soothing, gentle energy.

And as you find yourself relaxed in this way, try to sense or feel or imagine that there is a staircase before you. This staircase leads you closer to that place within you where you will make a connection with the power of the Great Mother. Now just allow yourself, as I count from ten to one, to travel along this staircase knowing that when I reach the number one you will be in that place where you will make a connection with the power of the Great Mother.

10 – Feeling your feet on the stair.

9 – Feeling your hand on the guardrail, knowing that you have complete control over this process.

8 – Knowing that if anything should become overwhelming for any reason, you can count yourself out from one to ten.

7 – Knowing that you can go quite deeply because you are so relaxed.

6 – Knowing that you can now let all of your inner senses open widely.

5 – Allowing your inner sense of taste, touch, smell, sight, hearing, and especially your sixth sense to open widely.

4 – And now bringing all of your inner senses and focusing them on a place, perhaps in nature, where you have felt comfortable and at peace.

3 – Knowing that you can let your conscious mind take a well-deserved rest as you focus on this place where you feel comfortable and at peace.

2 – Knowing that you can trust the impressions that you are receiving as you focus on this place where you feel comfortable and at peace.

1 – As you get to the end of the staircase, allow yourself to step out into this place. Take a deep breath in. Notice the quality of the light. Listen for any sounds. Notice if there is a breeze on your cheek or if the air is still. You may notice for the first time in a long time how much this place is a part of you and how much you are a part of this place. Just take a moment to feel this connection.

And then, even though it is so relaxing to be here again, I wonder if you can sense or feel or imagine that there is a path, a very inviting path, leading away from this place and leading you to the place where you will make a connection with the power of the Great Mother.

Now I am going to count from one to four. When I reach the number four, you will find yourself in the presence, or very close to being in the presence, of this part of yourself that you may perceive as a light, or sound, or animal, or teacher in human or plant form, or an angel or mythical being, or some other form that has special meaning for you.

1 – You find your feet on the path. Notice what the path is made of.

2 – Knowing that you will be able to talk to me loudly and clearly to describe your experience.

3 – Knowing that you can trust the impressions you are receiving and that your conscious mind can take a well-deserved rest.

4 – Now finding yourself in the presence or very close to the presence of the power of the Great Mother.

And as you feel the depth of your connection to this place, can you look around and sense or feel or imagine a presence, knowing that this presence is the power of the Great Mother? You may perceive this presence as a light or sound or animal or teacher in human or plant form or as an angel or mythical being—anything that has special meaning for you. And now, ask the power of the Great Mother "would you be willing to guide me and protect me?" You may receive this answer as a spoken or telepathic communication, or a change in the environment, or an action on the part of the power of the Great Mother, or an inner knowing. Again, ask the power of the Great Mother, "would you be willing to guide me and protect me?"

(Now is when the person being guided through the meditation can describe their experience. The experiences of many people at this moment in the meditation are described in chapter 8. Once the person is done speaking, continue guiding them through the closing of the meditation.)

Just letting yourself rest in this answer, knowing that more insights and understandings about the nature of this connection will come in the days ahead. But for now, with each number, make your connection with the power of the Great Mother stronger and deeper and wider.

1 – You feel the connection with the power of the Great Mother deeply.

2 – You are back on the staircase, returning along the same path to where you began.

3 – With each step you are moving closer to the surface.

4 – With each step, your connection with the power of the Great Mother is becoming more pronounced.

5 – You are halfway back along the staircase.

6 – You are beginning to feel the chair beneath you.

7 – You may want to stretch a bit.

8 – You are almost at the end of the staircase.

9 – Taking all the time you need, feel yourself coming back into the room.

10 – You reach the end of the staircase and are fully back in the room.

ACKNOWLEDGMENTS

As in traditional societies where children are parented by many adults, this book has been tended to by an entire village. Laura Chandler offered many hours of encouragement and support as she midwifed both the first and second edition with her insight and thoughtful edits. Melanie Robins has infused my words with her patient and inspired editing. Katie Rudman, Joanna Adler, and Simone Kershner have tirelessly proofed, re-read, and offered countless helpful suggestions. Cody Humston has tended to all the technical details. Wylie Nash offered her design expertise to the cover of the book. And so many of my students contributed accounts of their experiences of birth and of the Great Mother. I offer my deep appreciation to all of them for helping bring this book into the world. I offer endless thanks to the many initiates whose experiences are documented in this book and, of course, I extend my deepest gratitude to the Great Mother who has guided every aspect of the writing of this book.

BIBLIOGRAPHY

Aristizabal, Michelle. *Natural Labor and Birth: An Evidence-Based Guide to the Natural Birth Plan*. New York: McGraw Hill Education, 2019.

Block, Jennifer. *Pushed: The Painful Truth About Childbirth and Modern Maternity Care*. Cambridge, MA: Da Capo Press, 2007.

Campbell, Joseph. *The Hero with a Thousand Faces*. 3rd ed. Novato, CA: New World Library, 2008.

Connerton, W. C.. "Midwifery." *Encyclopedia Britannica*, May 25, 2012. https://www.britannica.com/science/midwifery.

Ehrenreich, Barbara and Deirdre English. *Witches, Midwives, & Nurses: A History of Women Healers*. New York: Feminist Press, 1973.

Epstein, Abby, director. *The Business of Being Born*. DVD. Burbank, CA: New Line Home Entertainment, 2008.

Gaskin, Ina May. *Ina May's Guide to Childbirth*. New York: Bantam Books, 2003.

Goldsmith, Judith. *Childbirth Wisdom: From the World's Oldest Societies*. New York: Closing the Circle Publications, 2019.

Grof, Stanislav. *Beyond the Brain: Birth, Death and Transcendence in Psychotherapy*. Albany: State University of New York Press, 1985.

Jones, Amy Cox. *The Way of the Peaceful Birther*. Springbrook, WI: Salt of the Earth Press, 2010.

Göttner-Abendroth, Heide. *Matriarchal Societies: Studies on Indigenous Cultures Across the Globe*. New York: Peter Lang Publishing, 2012.

Kinsley, David R. *Hindu Goddesses: Visions of the Divine Feminine in the Hindu Religious Tradition*. Berkeley: University of California Press, 1988.

Kline, Wendy. *Coming Home: How Midwives Changed Birth*. New York: Oxford University Press, 2021.

Lucas, Winafred Blake. *Regression Therapy: a Handbook for Professionals*. Crest Park, CA: Deep Forest Press, 1993.

MacDorman, Marian and Eugene Declercq. "Trends and State Variations in Out-of-Hospital Births in the United States, 2004-2017." *Birth* 46, no. 2 (2019), 279-288. doi: 10.1111/birt.12411.

Mariscotti de Gorlitz, Ana Maria. *Pachamama Santa Tierra: Estudia de la Religion Autoctona en los Andes Centro-meridionales*. Berlin: Mann, 1978.

Paul, Lois and Benjamin D. Paul. "*The Maya Midwife As Sacred Specialist: A Guatemalan Case*." *American Ethnologist* 2, no. 4 (1975): 707–726.

Reed, Ellen Cannon. *Circle of Isis: Ancient Egyptian Magic for Modern Witches*. Franklin Lakes, NJ: Career Press, 2002.

Rigoglioso, Marguerite. *Virgin Mother Goddesses of Antiquity*. New York: Palgrave Macmillan, 2010.

Sogyal Rinpoche. *The Tibetan Book of Living and Dying*. Edited by Patrick Gaffney and Andrew Harvey. San Francisco: HarperCollins, 1994.

Wertz, Richard W. and Dorothy C. Wertz. *Lying-In: A History of Childbirth in America*. expanded ed. New Haven: Yale University Press, 1989.

Williams, E. Leslie. *Spirit Tree: Origins of Cosmology in Shintô Ritual at Hakozaki*. Lanham, MD: University Press of America, 2007.

Waters, Frank. *Book of the Hopi*. New York: Penguin Books, 1977.

Willson, Martin. *In Praise of Tara: Songs to the Saviouress*. Boston: Wisdom Publications, 1996.

RESOURCES

Additional birth and initiation resources by Isa Gucciardi, Ph.D. available at sacredstream.org:

Great Mother Meditation (audio recording)
Preparing for an Empowered Birth (audio recording)
Initiations of the Sacred Feminine (workshop)
Tracking Spirit in the Birth Environment: The Creative Portal (workshop)

For more information, visit isagucciardi.org and depthhypnosis.org.

ABOUT THE AUTHOR

Isa Gucciardi, Ph.D. is the founding director of the Foundation of the Sacred Stream, a school for consciousness studies located in Berkeley, CA. She teaches and speaks nationally and internationally and is the author of *Coming to Peace* and the forthcoming *Depth Hypnosis: a Path to Inner Transformation*. She maintains a private practice with institutions and individuals engaged in Depth Hypnosis and Coming to Peace processes. Isa speaks five languages and has lived in eleven countries. She is the mother of two children and lives with her partner in San Francisco.

Made in the USA
Monee, IL
02 September 2021

77159564R00056